To

George H. Weiss

this volume is inscribed
with the cordial regards of
the compiler,

Isabella Scott
December 24, 1928.

Shakespeare

© Aitken

Shakespeare

SHAKESPEARE

WRITINGS OF
HARVEY W. SCOTT
LATE EDITOR OF THE
MORNING OREGONIAN

Compiled by
LESLIE M. SCOTT

CAMBRIDGE
PRINTED AT THE RIVERSIDE PRESS
1928

Preface

HARVEY W. SCOTT, editor of the Portland *Oregonian*, read daily the dramas of Shakespeare, whom he considered the leading moralist and the foremost thinker of his time, as well as the greatest writer of English.

Mr. Scott, through forty years of newspaper life, produced an editorial page which was widely known for literary vigor and variety. This work drew upon the best resources of his thinking, and turned him to the 'oceanic mind' of Shakespeare. His favorite commentaries on the 'myriad-minded' dramatist are included in this book.

The compiler has sought to show that the Stratford master of English may aid a modern writer. In this spirit the volume in hand is submitted to general readers, and particularly to members of the publishing craft.

The compiler is indebted to Miss E. Ruth Rockwood, head of the reference department of the Library Association of Portland, Ore-

gon, and to the department, Queries and An-
swers, of *The New York Times*, for valuable
assistance in locating the sources of literary
allusions used by Mr. Scott. Acknowledg-
ments are also due to Dr. Luella Clay Car-
son, of Los Angeles, California, formerly
Professor of English in the University of
Oregon and afterwards president of Mills
College, California, for reading of proofs;
and to Mr. Robert Aitken, of New York
City, sculptor, for permission to use his
portrait of Shakespeare as the frontispiece of
this volume.

THE COMPILER

PORTLAND, OREGON
February 1, 1928

Contents

PART II. AUTHORSHIP OF SHAKESPEARE

PART III. MISCELLANY ON SHAKESPEARE

PART I
GENIUS OF SHAKESPEARE

Shakespeare's Impersonal Authorship

From The Oregonian, December 4, 1904

GREATEST literature is in the dramatic form; so, in all countries and in all ages. In our time the drama is not striking; so, literature is not. But it would be unwise to conclude that the dramatic power is exhausted. Under new conditions, that power has revived through thousands of years, although at long intervals. And, judged from this long experience, it will revive again.

Even in forms of literature not purely dramatic, nor written with reference to the stage, but only for the reader, the dramatic parts, wherein the author makes the speaker or the person represented do the work, carry the interest and passion over the descriptive and narrative parts, which, indeed, constitute but the framework, to be filled by dramatic recital. The chief interest of the great epic poems and of the great novels, and even of the great historical works, lies in the play of feeling through the dramatic parts. The actor speaks from nature.

As Shakespeare is the first dramatist of the world, so he is incomparably the first writer; and the first thinker, also. But the best work of this kind is purely impersonal. The reader, the hearer, the spectator, must be on his guard against the supposition that he is getting the author's opinions.

Immense labor has been devoted to the effort to develop Shakespeare's religious opinions, from passages in his dramas; but the labor comes to little, because this writer was so entirely impersonal. Shakespeare had intuitive knowledge of the dramatic art and spirit, above all persons who ever lived; he is the mirror, through which is reflected the natural spirit of his own creations. One is not reading such a writer's opinions when one reads Shakespeare.

The human spirit displays itself naturally in the dramatic form of literature. In the hands of a master, each person speaks according to his own nature; and the ordinary character is enlivened with all the wit and wisdom, or again, is represented with all the stupidities or other limitations, belonging naturally to the situation. The author, who attempts to interject his own personality, fails. He writes prosy tragedies or dull comedies, instead of masterpieces. The author, dealing entirely with a situation in which others act, but in which he is not an actor, must be unconscious of himself. Herein is the reason why writers, like Johnson and Dryden and Young and Tennyson, all of whom tried the drama, never could do much with it. In their efforts, we have only the writer, and his own feelings and opinions; not the creations of a boundless sympathy and imagination, supported by an observant mind. Therefore, it is impossible to obtain the personal opinions of a great dramatist from his written works.

We have spoken of Shakespeare's religious opinions. The question is, perhaps, of small importance. Yet, everything connected with the life of this genius of writers and thinkers has some interest. A man, who was either a narrow skeptic or a bitter sectarian, could not have displayed the large-hearted humanity shown in the plays of Shakespeare, nor the psychologic power, dominated by morality, shown in his sonnets; and although it is not probable that he was in the least fanatical in his views, his nature, as revealed through his works, was essentially religious. There is a tolerance everywhere in his works that is remarkable; and it has been shown by one and another, to their own satisfaction, that he was a Catholic, an Anglican and an agnostic. Here and there we find a little satire directed against the Puritan, but it is never mordant. No one can say that Shakespeare was either Catholic or Protestant; and, although passages of so-called 'unquestioned Protestantism' have been pointed out in *Henry VIII*, the lines undoubtedly belong to Fletcher, who collaborated with Shakespeare in this, as in *The Two Noble Kinsmen* and other plays. If any character was drawn by the dramatist with a loving hand, it is Henry V; and he is a well-nigh perfect type of Catholic hero. Henry V, in Shakespeare's pages, is profoundly religious, in a Catholic sense. Elsewhere, Shakespeare constantly made reference to distinctly Catholic doctrines and practices — prayers for the dead, fasting, penance, pious foundations and the religious life, yet often without the precision of a devout Catholic.

Again, in *Hamlet*, he produced one of the grand skeptical dramas of the world although competitors are the *Book of Job*, *Prometheus Bound*, of Æschylus, and *Faust*, of Goethe. All his work is full of religious folklore, as of all other folklore, which is used universally for illustration, or as framework or support of statement, argument or feeling, but without the slightest touch of prejudice, intolerance or sneer. Shakespeare is the only writer, save Homer, who spoke with absolute impersonality, through the characters he has created. He who has come next to these, strange to say, is the author of that immortal burlesque and satire, *Don Quixote*.

Shakespeare's Problems of Life and Mind

From The Oregonian, August 14, 1909

ONE who fails to understand Shake-speare cannot enter Shakespeare's world; which is the widest intellectual and moral and spiritual world yet revealed to the sons and daughters of men. This is the test: If one cannot understand Shakespeare, it is because one is too narrow; has not range enough.

On the religious side, the old Hebrew prophets have the like expression; and, since religion and morals have close relation and each supports the other, the Hebrew Scriptures are the highest expression of the religious emotions and moral aspirations of mankind. Their sacredness over other writings is another subject.

Charles W. Eliot, whose selections for his 'five-foot shelf of books'[1] contains not one

[1] Dr. Eliot's 'five-foot shelf of books,' published in *Harvard Classics*, contains *Hamlet, King Lear, Macbeth* and *The Tempest*; also *Job, Psalms, Ecclesiastes, Gospel of Luke, Acts of the Apostles* and Paul's *Epistle to the Corinthians.*

which the world could spare, did not at
first include in his list Shakespeare and the
Bible. He doubts that either can be read
understandingly, without high culture. All
the more necessary, then, is high culture.
There are others, besides Shakespeare. But
he is supreme. Others, indeed, are mighty,
when Shakespeare's face is hid.

To string out quotations and comments in
order to show that Shakespeare is the first,
not only of observers and thinkers, but also
of moral writers, would be the easiest of
undertakings. He had wider range of observation and experience than the Hebrew
writers, and his thought had modern proofs
for support. Hence his peculiar power. He
was a prodigy. There are no miracles; and
prodigies appear only in the intellectual and
moral world. There is nothing that much
astonishes the world in the appearance of a
new potato or cherry. But no one expects
another Isaiah or Shakespeare or Molière or
Milton. Men may appear again whose power
will astonish the world, but they will not
be like those who have preceded. It is, of
course, impossible to set limits to human
powers. But no one can see how there ever

can be another great poet like Homer or
Shakespeare or Tasso or Milton, or another
great conqueror like Napoleon. Yet, there
may be more possibility of a Napoleon than
of a Shakespeare.

How Account for
Shakespeare?

From The Oregonian, February 20, 1910

ONE of the latest productions of
Algernon Charles Swinburne was
an essay on Shakespeare, recently
published. With this poet's earlier *A Study
of Shakespeare* (1880) and *The Age of Shakespeare* (1908), the reading world is familiar.
This latest essay begins thus:

> There is one book in the world, of
> which it might be affirmed and argued,
> without fear of derision from any but
> the supreme and crowning fools among
> the foolishest of mankind, that it would
> be better for the world to lose all others
> and keep this one, than to lose this and
> keep all other treasures bequeathed by
> human genius to all that we can con-
> ceive of eternity, to all that we can con-
> ceive of immortality. That book is best
> known, and best described for all of us,
> simply by the simple English name of
> its author. The word Shakespeare con-
> notes more than any other man's name

that ever was written or spoken upon earth.

One scarcely could have expected Swinburne to write this, since it is so true as to be commonplace. Likewise, this remark farther on: 'All that can be known of mankind, of womanhood and of childhood, he knew better than any man ever born.' Of *Hamlet*, in this latest essay, Swinburne wrote:

> The greatest of Shakespeare's tragedies 'tis not; but it is not unintelligible that it should pass for such in general and traditional estimation. The infinite and imperishable charm of the leading character, in all its mystery and all its actuality, is wider in the universal attraction of its appeal than that of any other among the creatures of the omnipotence of Shakespeare.

This is well said; the discrimination is excellent. According to Swinburne's judgment, *A Midsummer Night's Dream*, in comedy, and *King Lear*, in tragedy, stand at top of value in Shakespeare's work. In this judgment many will agree, but not all; for *Henry IV* and *Macbeth* probably appeal to

more. Again, there are those who cannot
place *As You Like It* and *Romeo and Juliet*
after any other dramas.

A new and, so far as we know, an original
judgment on the method and range of
Shakespeare, is a book entitled *The Man
Shakespeare and His Tragic Life Story*
(1909), by Frank Harris. This writer is not
known to the large world of readers, but is
a man of letters and a journalist of distinc-
tion;[1] and his essay on Shakespeare is ob-
taining attention on both sides of the Atlantic. His view is different from that of
Swinburne and from that of Coleridge,
since he does not accept the oracular and
idolatrous dictum of the supreme poet, as
Matthew Arnold said of him:

> Thou smilest and art still,
> Out-topping knowledge.

Swinburne takes Hamlet as a type-char-
acter, revealing the leading quality of
Shakespeare's mind and spirit, and finds his
greatest creations, throughout all the plays,
a subtle variation of the Hamlet type. From
a review of Mr. Harris' book in *The Forum*

[1] Also author of *The Women of Shakespeare* (1911).

for February, 1910, page 202, we make this extract:

> Mr. Harris affirms that Hamlet is Shakespeare's first complete portrait of himself, and proceeds both to apply his theory and to prove the Hamlet-Shakespeare identity, by finding trait after trait of Hamlet in a multitude of other characters. Now, the Hamlet traits are well known: Introspection, irresolution, pessimism, scholarliness, melancholy, garrulity, sensuousness and sensualism — these are but a partial catalogue. A moment's consideration, with the help of Mr. Harris' skillful quotation, shows that most of them are present in Romeo, a character limned some eleven years before Hamlet. Temperamentally, Romeo is a 'younger brother of Hamlet,' although like Jaques, another early portrait, merely a pale reflection. But it is in Macbeth that we find the closest parallels. The chapter in which the startling analogy between Macbeth and Hamlet is clearly and persuasively drawn, is undoubtedly the most brilliant bit in the book. Macbeth is simply Hamlet over again, with every trait repeated and emphasized. Shakespeare's powers have increased in the brief interval between the two plays; striving to

portray Macbeth's innermost self, he
unconsciously falls into self-portrayal,
and gives us that series of concise
monologues whose definite individuality
stands in striking contrast to Hamlet's
rambling incoherencies. Macbeth is as
incapable of action as Hamlet was;
by nature meditative, introspective and
religious, he is totally unsuited to the
plot at hand. Whenever he is called
upon to act, he must be nerved up to the
deed by Lady Macbeth's fierce prompt-
ings, or by a courage temporarily in-
stilled by a torturing monologue.

This extract is sufficient to convey an idea
of the main theory of the essay. Minor
characters in Shakespeare are considered
as persons who, lacking an individuality of
their own, yet embracing the general variety
that had fallen under the poet's keen observation, were merely the mouthpieces of
his quick and ready thought. But Mr. Harris has a theory of his own, as to the source
of the melancholy mood of greatest Shakespearean characters. He thinks he finds it
in sonnet No. 42, from which he construes
a revelation of a disappointed lover, who
sends a friend to do his wooing, only to be
betrayed, and loses both friend and maid:

If I lose thee, my loss is my love's gain,
And losing her, my friend hath found that
 loss;
Both find each other, and I lose both twain,
And both for my sake lay on me this cross.

The sonnets always have been an enigma of literature; and one who studies them, under this suggestion, scarcely can deem the interpretation purely fanciful, or lacking an element of strong probability. And yet, although Shakespeare has been discussed for three centuries, as no mortal ever was, who can say with sureness, or predict with certainty, that it ever will be possible to pluck the heart out of the mystery?

Shakespeare and Sacred English

From The Oregonian, September 18, 1887

IN *The Church Review* for September, 1887 (Episcopalian), Appleton Morgan[1] contributes a valuable article, 'Shakespearean English and the Prayer Book,' in which, from comparison of Shakespeare with the Prayer Book and King James version of the Bible, it is shown that there are similarities in the use of words, which are found in no other literature of the time; also, that the concordances to the King James version and to the Shakespeare works almost might be used interchangeably.

The conclusions are reduced to the following statements: (1) That the King James translators, in searching for a true vernacular that should be as permanent and as widely intelligible as possible, went to the English of the Prayer Book; (2) that what

[1] Author of various commentaries on Shakespeare. See pages 99-104, following.

they brought thence was just what William Shakespeare had already brought from somewhere and converted to his own use; (3) that the product which the two, translators and Shakespeare, have presented to us as their own, is practically unused and unclaimed by their contemporaries.

Given this statement of facts, if they be facts, what are we to devise therefrom as to the probability of a source? What else than that their source was a common one; that it was the liturgy of the English church which dominated the one, as it dominated the other, and so supplied the long-searched-for and subjective originals of the English of Shakespeare?

Light is thrown on this interesting subject by George P. Marsh's *Lectures on the English Language.* Part of his plan was an inquiry into the origin of the remarkable language of our English Bible. This he traced as a stream of language parallel with the general current of English speech, but having a sacred character. This sacred language of English came down from Wycliffe, and probably had remote sources even beyond Wycliffe. In Shakespeare's day, it was as accessible to all others as to Shakespeare, but he alone had the power to use it as an instrument of general composition. But one archer could bend that bow.

Folklore of Shakespeare

From The Oregonian, April 19, 1885

THE term *folklore* is of recent origin, and stands in literature for that which is as old as literature itself. It signifies the tales, legends, traditions and superstitions of a people; their ideas upon common and uncommon things; their sayings and proverbs illustrative of the life around them. In this kind of lore, no writer is so rich as Shakespeare. Long ago, in 1767, Richard Farmer demonstrated, and the labors of others have confirmed his conclusions, that Shakespeare, despite all that the commentators, doctors, lawyers, ornithologists, entomologists, botanists and other specialists find, or pretend to find in his work, was anything but a man of learning. Shakespeare had —

> small Latin and less Greek,[1]

says Jonson, and had but a smattering of French. Even of English literature, other than what was contemporary, he was no

[1] See page 85, following.

profound student, although he seems to have read with some attention both Chaucer and the older chronicles.

But, although Shakespeare had little learning, he had incomparable knowledge. His mind assimilated the very marrow of the books he read, and, above all, seized upon what was likely to be serviceable in his profession of playwright. His genius was not the predominance of one faculty, but the predominance of all faculties. He was as accurate as he was a keen observer, whether concerned with a country, custom or legend, with a craftsman's detail, with a fact of nature or with a mental or emotional phase. He was never diffuse. If we eliminate from his plays some portions addressed to the gallery, scarcely a line will be found not bearing upon the development of the action of the drama. Having the richest imagination and a boundless fertility, he was hardly tempted to use an extravagant epithet or to resort to an overstrained metaphor or an unnecessary illustration. The ordinary facts of human experience, in their passage through his brain, were transmuted, as in an alembic, into pure gold.

Folklore is not in itself poetical, although it may come to appear so as civilization moves men farther from their origin. Of the materials that lay in Shakespeare's hand, the contemporary folklore was among the commonest. But it was abundant and varied, and full of potential poetry, which his genius unfolded in adapting to his purposes. For an unlearned public, no better illustration could be drawn than from such a source. It is partly on this ground, partly by reason of the scantiness of his learning, that Shakespeare, who was troubled by no such considerations of a quasi-classical dignity as hampered the French dramatists of a succeeding age, made so extensive and unexampled a use of the folklore current in his day.

Shakespeare's Favorite Hero

From The Oregonian, September 3, 1887

THE five-hundredth anniversary of the birth of the great warrior king, Henry V, recently was celebrated in England with brilliant commemorative pageantry. England does not commemorate the birth of Alfred, a far greater king, whose victories were in the direction of peace, enlarged learning and civilization; England does not notice the birthday of Edward III, or that of his great son, Edward, the Black Prince, although between them the French were —

in their own land beaten, bobb'd and thump'd,

(the words are those of King Richard III) as severely as by the victor of Agincourt.

Edward IV, as great a warrior as Henry V, is consigned to oblivion for the same reason as Oliver Cromwell, because he was the victor in a great civil war; and, at the restoration of the heirs of the Lancastrian kings, no honors were paid to the memory of the victor of Towton and Barnet.

But why does the figure of Henry V remain, five centuries after his birth, the favorite subject of commemorative honors, rather than Edward III and his great son? The historic Henry V is not a large nor a noble figure, historically. He was a man of military talents, but he was not a statesman, like his father, Henry IV, nor was he a man of the generous and chivalrous impulses that not seldom characterized Edward III and his son, in the hour of victory. He was a hardy, intensely ambitious military chieftain, of cold, selfish, cruel temper. He persecuted the Wycliffites, or Lollards, with barbarity, whom his grandfather, John of Gaunt, had always protected, and cruelly put to death their leader, Sir John Oldcastle, who had been his intimate friend and a gallant and loyal soldier of the crown in the civil wars of his father, Henry IV.

Henry V began his reign with the execution of the Earl of Cambridge, whose son, as Duke of York, avenged his father by dethroning Henry VI; and he undertook the war with France, largely to divert the minds of the great warrior nobles from the contemplation of insurrection. His career was brief, brilliant and barbarous, even for his day. A sober soldier, not a voluptuary like Edward III and Edward IV, he was a harsh master and a cruel victor over France. His lack of statesmanship was shown by his French marriage, which he executed against the advice of his wise brother, Bedford, who urged him to make an English marriage that would cement his authority at home, instead of exciting needless prejudice by the other course.

This, in brief, is the historic Henry V, whose birthday is commemorated in England. Clearly, he was merely a rude soldier of exceptional military talents and merciless temper; in no sense a sagacious statesman or a man of large and chivalrous soul. His career was calamitous to England, for the direct consequence of his wasteful French wars was a state of chronic turbulence and discontent at home which resulted, after his death, in a civil war.

The hero of Agincourt continues to-day to be a popular figure in the gallery of England's heroes, because the fascinating figure of Prince Hal, given by Shakespeare to the dramatic stage, has come to be accepted as the true picture of the victor of Agincourt. Ruskin calls Henry V the one entirely heroic man in all Shakespeare's plays. Prince Hal has wit, humor, good nature, valor, generosity, magnanimity and good sense, underneath the superficial wildness of his early youth; his great parts stand out in salient strength, whenever a great occasion calls him to the front; in his lightest, most careless and indolent hours, when he is playing with Falstaff and using him for laughter, he cannot be mistaken for a weak man, or a bad man. There is no taste of vulgarity or sensuality in him; he drinks and listens to Falstaff's witty sallies, just as Hawthorne used to drink claret and listen for hours to the racy talk of the sea captains, on the docks at Salem and Marblehead. Prince Hal never loses his dignity, even when he seems to permit familiarity.

Promptly and sternly, with a word, he brings all his boon companions to a deferential mood, when they carry their trifling too far. When he becomes king, his language is that of a humane statesman and philosopher, as he talks in disguise with his soldiers the night before the battle. When he addresses his army, how splendid and inspiring is his speech; how heroic his spirit! What a contrast between Henry V's noble words to his army before Agincourt, and Richard III's ferocious, sullen growl before Bosworth! Richard speaks like Macbeth, a very valiant villain and murderer at bay, while Henry, in *Henry V*, speaks like a soldier, of the serene courage and purity of Chevalier de Bayard:

He that outlives this day, and comes safe home,
Will stand a-tiptoe when this day is named.
And rouse him at the name of Crispian.
He that shall live this day, and see old age,
Will yearly on the vigil feast his neighbors,
And say, 'To-morrow is Saint Crispian.'
Then will he strip his sleeve and show his scars,
And say, 'These wounds I had on Crispian's day.'
Old men forget; yet all shall be forgot,
But he'll remember with advantages
What feats he did that day; then shall 'our
      names,'
Familiar in his mouth as household words,
Be in their flowing cups freshly remembered.
This story shall the good man teach his son;

        *   *   *

From this day to the ending of the world,
But we in it shall be remembered;

        *   *   *

And gentlemen in England now a-bed
Shall think themselves accursed they were not
    here,
And hold their manhoods cheap whiles any
    speaks
That fought with us upon Saint Crispian's day.

This noble, dramatic figure, drawn by Shakespeare, has usurped in the popular mind, by frequent stage representation, the memory of the real Henry, but the true portrait is known to the veracious historian.

Feminism in Shakespeare's Plays

From The Oregonian, September 22, 1895

IT is one of the commonplaces of commentary on Shakespeare, that his women are always feminine. But that requires us to forget Lady Macbeth and Tamora. A recent writer lays much stress on the assumption that the great dramatist never made a woman the leading character in a play. Sometimes, it is said, he made the man and the woman joint stars, as Romeo and Juliet, Macbeth and Lady Macbeth, Benedict and Beatrice; but he never violated what this writer calls nature, by making the woman the dramatic unit. This statement, however, is subject to even more exceptions than the other, that his women are always feminine.

Is not Rosalind as much the dramatic unit in _As You Like It_, as Hamlet is in the play that bears his name? Does not Viola rule in _Twelfth Night_, and is not Isabella, in _Measure for Measure_, the person without whom the play would be nothing? In one case we have woman's wit; in another, woman's love; in the third, woman's moral convictions, as the mainspring of the play. Are not some of Shakespeare's women, then, more than the corresponding men?

But we may say that, while we hardly know what the new woman is, it seems that Shakespeare did not know, either; for he has not created any woman that could furnish an outline for this modern character. He made, indeed, many of his women assume male attire, but we do not see the modern new woman in one of them. They make but a poor figure in *As You Like It*, in putting on —

a swashing and a martial outside.

Rosalind, perhaps the most boisterous of all the fine women that the great dramatist caused to assume man's attire, confesses that, though dressed like a man, she has no doublet and hose in her disposition. The modesty of Imogen and of Viola is so true to the highest types of womanhood, that it almost escapes one, while reading the plays or seeing them acted, that these women assumed the disguise of man's dress. They had the outward, but not the inward doublet and hose. That is, the wizard of human nature showed, three centuries ago, how woman could assume the dress of man without loss of those qualities which the world esteems as distinctly feminine.

We confess incredulity about the new woman of to-day and her possible existence, because Shakespeare did not foreknow her.

Shakespeare's A Divine Thrusting on

From The Oregonian, September 3, 1887

SOME writer,' says the *Pacific Christian Advocate* (Methodist), 'has used this very expressive phrase to describe a life that does not go of its own volition merely, but by the force of divine impulse and in accordance with the divine plan.' The writer is Shakespeare, but the *Advocate* is in error in the application. In *King Lear*, Gloster says:

> These late eclipses in the sun and moon portend no good to us; though the wisdom of nature can reason it thus and thus, yet nature finds itself scourged by the sequent effects. Love cools, friendship falls off, brothers divide; in cities, mutinies; in country, discord; in palaces, treason, and the bond cracked 'twixt son and father.

The speech goes on much further in the same strain. Then follows Edmund's reply:

> This is the excellent foppery of the

world, that, when we are sick in fortune
(often the surfeit of our own behavior),
we make guilty of our disasters the sun,
the moon and the stars; as if we were
villains by necessity; fools by heavenly
compulsion; knaves, thieves and treach-
ers by spherical predominance; drunkards, liars and adulterers by enforced
obedience of planetary influence, and all
that we are evil in, by a divine thrusting on.

The lesson of this speech is quite the op-
posite of that which the *Advocate* would find,
in the single expression it quotes. Although
the speech is put in the mouth of a villain,
it contains a protest of everlasting truth
against the pretense that man is not mor-
ally responsible for his own conduct. It is
the instinct of human nature to evade this
responsibility, to throw the burden of one's
deviation from the line of rectitude on influences that control the man in spite of himself. The fault is anywhere, everywhere, but
in the individual's own inclination to go
wrong. When it can be placed nowhere else,
it is charged to the bend sinister given the
man by his Maker; the man falls into evil
ways through 'a divine thrusting on,' which

of course he is powerless to resist, and his poverty, wretchedness, crime, infamy and death —

often the surfeit of our own behavior,

as Edmund says in *King Lear*, are all the results, in this false philosophy, of the operation of forces and circumstances which turn the man to destruction, and of which he is the victim, without fault of his own. Does he turn thief? He has been ill-used and driven to theft. Does he turn drunkard? The liquor seller is the one at fault. Does he murder a woman who declines his addresses? The divine power of love has overcome him. Has he wasted his substance in lewd and riotous living? Bad women are to blame. And the worst of all this is the even more pernicious philosophy, that goes as counterpart, taught by professed reformers, that the way to avert these consequences is not by subduing the evil propensities in the man's nature, by teaching him his own responsibility and building him up in moral strength, but by abolishing the things to which he attributes his fall.

From The Oregonian, January 4, 1869

For the sake of safety and justice, we should stifle misdirected sympathy with guilty offenders. Shakespeare, in *Measure for Measure*, thus described the consequences of laxity in enforcement of law:

> Now, as fond fathers,
> Having bound up the threatening twigs of birch,
> Only to stick it in their children's sight
> For terror, not to use; in time the rod
> Becomes more mock'd than fear'd; so our de-
>   crees,
> Dead to inflection, to themselves are dead,
> And liberty plucks justice by the nose.

It is indefensible that there should be sympathy with one who takes human life, based on the idea that the victim is a person of no consequence. Yet there are frequent indications of such sympathy.

From The Oregonian, May 6, 1884

Prompt trial and swift execution of the death penalty, is the sharpest and best medicine to cure a cutthroat; the grave is a prison more frightful to the ordinary assassin than even the living death of life imprisonment, whose cell is never so dark but is lighted by that ray of hope we call executive pardon. Shakespeare sketched, with truthful hand, the horror exercised on the average mind by the death penalty, when he wrote, in *Measure for Measure:*

> The weariest and most loathed worldly life
> That age, ache, penury and imprisonment
> Can lay on nature is a paradise
> To what we fear of death.

Shakespeare sounded human nature deeply, on this as on all other subjects — more deeply than do those who affirm that, because the death penalty does not deter some men from murder, it does not deter any possible murderers from crime, and that, therefore, we would do well to dismantle the gallows.

Spontaneity of Shakespeare

From The Oregonian, October 2, 1887

T is probable that Milton's poetic powers were —

       cabin'd, cribb'd, confin'd,

(the quoted words are Macbeth's), if not crippled, by his scholarship. Milton justly is placed next to Shakespeare, and yet it is not an extravagant supposition to believe that Shakespeare, had he received the severe scholastic training of Milton, would have been crippled for his loftiest flights, just as an Oxford training probably would have taken all the scent of simple Scottish human nature out of Burns, and made him a poet of human society rather than of human nature.

Much has been written concerning the automatic or unconscious powers of the human mind. Their work has been illustrated by the old legend of the beneficent goblin,[1] who was the attendant of some

---

[1] 'Lubber fiend,' in Milton's *L'Allegro*, 110; 'Farewell, thou lob of spirits,' the fairy to Puck in *A Midsummer Night's Dream*, II, 116; 'Lob lie-by-the-fire,' in Fletcher's *Knight of the Burning Pestle.*

favored mortal, and who, when that mortal's ordinary hour of activity was over and he was sleeping, went on with the mortal's uncompleted task, so that the man rose in the bright sunlight, to find his house swept and garnished by invisible hands that, after doing their work wisely and well, had followed the wings of the first morning and silently stolen away. This illustration has been applied variously to the work that the unconscious powers of the human mind do for the conscious powers, when their day of labor is over in the separate realms of memory, reason and the purely emotional nature of man. The unconscious powers, like the lover fiend's invisible service, are the illimitable, impalpable, shadowy feeders of the conscious powers. The highest type of the human mind is unconsciousness of effort. All really great men in song, music, story, art — in short, all the geniuses, whether contemplative or practical, have approached this type of unconsciousness, the wisdom that does not think of being wise; the ability that does not aim to be able. The higher the quality of genius, the larger the copiousness of the conscious powers, the more fertile and

wonderful the exhibition of the unconscious
powers.

The domain of memory affords a familiar
and full field of illustration of the mind's
unconscious powers. Memory, more perhaps than the creative or inventive faculty,
feeds the orator and poet. So indeterminate
are the obligations to unconscious memory,
that Plato was persuaded to believe his
thoughts were but the representatives of his
past soul life, whether of this life or of a
state of preëxistence. Sir Walter Scott, dictating one sentence while he composed the
next; Canning and Napoleon, dictating to
their secretaries in turn on three different
subjects, have been quoted as illustrations
of the automatic reasoning powers of the
human mind.

Now, granting, as we must, the extraordinary genius of the author of Shakespeare's plays, his powers covered a restless,
boundless activity of both the conscious and
the unconscious mind, to which our ordinary
realm of consciousness is but a landlocked
harbor, and this capacity for conscious and
unconscious activity, at any time and at all
times, bubbling constantly like a great

spring, exhaustless because it reaches back to the immensity of the earth, is the marvel of Shakespeare. He was the effortless, unconscious man of genius; the incarnation of the most superb spontaneity of soul, heart and intellect. Such a man easily might go astray, in his ignorance of geography, history and chronology, but in the domain of the emotional nature, love, sympathy, the passionate spirituality of the affections, or in the realm of the purely spiritual, where, as in Addison's *Cato*, act V, scene I —

'Tis the divinity that stirs within us;
'Tis heaven itself, that points out an hereafter,
And intimates eternity to man,

there, Shakespeare never lost himself; there, he surveyed his empire and beheld his intellectual home.

And 'a Babbled of Green Fields

From The Oregonian, December 13, 1896

FANCIFUL theories, in the interpretation and criticism of authors, receive new illustration in the discussion about the source and meaning of Dame Quickly's phrase:

And 'a babbled of green fields,

in her account of Falstaff's death, in *Henry V.*

Mr. Locke Richardson, in *The Critic*, offers the theory that the passage in the Twenty-third Psalm, 'He maketh me to lie down in green pastures,' was the source of the expression.[1]

The mind of Shakespeare moved with inconceivable rapidity. It is often difficult, sometimes impossible, to follow the movements. Upon every page, the reader notes flashes, produced, of course, by the working of an incomparable mind; but, in instances innumerable, neither the process nor the

---

[1] The article in *The Critic*, November 28, 1896, is accompanied by comments, written by William J. Rolfe and Horace Howard Furness who speak kindly of Mr. Richardson's ingenuity and deprecate mildly his explanation.

material is discoverable. The subtlety and power of the work give a result that is un-exampled for originality and effect, and it is not surprising that the search for the original form of the material eludes every effort of discovery.

Mr. Richardson's interpretation of 'and 'a babbled of green fields' seems fanciful. They who try to find what was in the mind of the author, commonly reveal only some pecu-liarity of their own minds. Through this process, it is easy to find resemblances where none in fact exists.

The history of this passage will show that the attempt to identify it with a passage of the Twenty-third Psalm, is but a conjecture founded upon a conjecture. It is not certain that Shakespeare wrote 'and 'a babbled of green fields,' but very probable that he did not.

The old copy, that is, the first folio, the first collected edition of Shakespeare's plays, brought out by his affectionate associates, Heming and Condell, in 1623, seven years after Shakespeare's death, reads, in *Henry V* at this place:

For after I saw him fumble with the

> sheets, and play with flowers, and smile
> upon his finger's end, I knew there was
> but one way; for his nose was as sharp
> as a pen on a table of green fields.

These last words are nonsense. The change
to "a babbled of green fields' was a conjectural emendation made by Theobald, a
century later.[1] It must be admitted that it
was happy, but it is only a guess, and has
nothing to support it but the fact that it is an
improvement, that fits well with the general
text.

In the earlier editions of this play, the
words, 'and a table of green fields,' printed
in the first folio of 1623, did not appear.
Three earlier editions are known, those of
1600, 1602 and 1608. In these editions the
end of the sentence was 'for his nose was
sharp as a pen.' How came the additional
words, 'and a table of green fields,' in the
first folio, the edition of Heming and Condell, of 1623, and in the successive folio
editions of 1632, 1663 and 1685? Pope
omitted the words from his *The Works of
Shakespeare* (1725), and said:

[1] Suggested by a marginal conjecture in an edition of
Shakespeare 'by a gentleman sometime deceased'; Theobald's
Shakespeare Restored (1726).

These words, *and a table of green fields*, are not to be found in the old editions of 1600 and 1608. This nonsense got into all the following editions by the pleasant mistake of stage editors, who printed from the common piecemeal-written parts of the playhouse. A table was here directed to be brought in (it being a scene in a tavern where they drink at parting), and this direction crept into the text from the margin. Greenfield was the name of the property man in that time, who furnished the implements, etc., for the actors. 'A table from Greenfield's.'[1]

Pope did not refer to the sources of his knowledge, and some of the eminent critics have accepted his explanation, while others have not. But it is a reasonable account of the origin of the passage; and in view of the absence of the words from the early editions, of the first appearance in the edition of 1623, and of the fact that the emendation, 'and 'a babbled of green fields,' is but a conjectural attempt of a century later to make a meaning for a nonsensical passage that in some way crept into the first folio, it would seem

[1] See William Aldis Wright's *The Works of Shakespeare*, Cambridge edition, 1903, IV, 712, note.

that there is small reason to go into ecstasies over the supposed theory, that resemblance to a passage in the Twenty-third Psalm accounts for the origin. Shakespeare abounds in subtle allusions to the Scriptures, as to everything else written, known or imagined, down to his time; but Pope's explanation about 'a table from Greenfield's,' taken in connection with the known history of the play and the manners of the time, it appears to us, should moderate the raptures of those who hail this discovery. These excessive refinements of critical interpretations, built on hypotheses that themselves may be built on conjectures or blunders, are edifying sometimes for their absurdities; yet often they have a real value; not, indeed, for their actual results, but for the fact that they tend to sharpen and to improve the methods of criticism.

Shakespeare's Familiar yet Hard Lessons

From The Oregonian, July 25, 1905

IT is bad business for a man to marry a woman much older than himself. In such alliance nothing fits. Disgust or indifference is likely to arise on the one side, and jealousy on the other. The true object of marriage is the making of a home and the rearing of children. Happy harmony between husband and wife is the indispensable condition of this realization. Shakespeare gave as good advice on many matters of life, as we find in holy writ; and better, in some instances, because it proceeds from the experience of modern life. This passage, in *Twelfth Night*, for one:

> Let still the woman take
> An elder than herself; so wears she to him,
> So sways she level in her husband's heart.

Nothing more is needed on this subject. It is the last word. Likewise, on intermarriage of the races. Let the tragedy of *Othello* stand for that lesson.

And, for a lesson on the folly of those who, in their advanced years, give away their property or estate and expect others, even their own children, to care for them, one should read and never forget *King Lear*.

Examples of all these mistakes are occurring, continually. In the daily reports presented through the newspapers, they follow in steady train. They tread each other's heel, throughout the year. What seems to be new under the sun is reappearance, mostly, of new incidents of old experience. Yet, withal, it is hard to learn the lessons.

Usury *vs.* Interest in Shakespeare's Day

From The Oregonian, November 16, 1891

THE idea, that the lending of money upon interest is wrong, is deeply embedded in the Old and the New Testaments. There, interest on money uniformly is called 'usury,' and is almost always strongly denounced. The idea still survived very generally, when the current English version of the Bible was made. Shakespeare does not know the word *interest*, as a term signifying a sum paid for the use of money; but 'usury' is a common word with him, and, in most cases, is used in a sense which makes plain that what we now call *interest* was in his time still looked upon with general disfavor. It was monstrous, many said, that money, being a barren thing, should be made to breed money. Bacon had this idea; so had Sir Matthew Hale.

> For when did friendship take
> A breed for barren metal of his friend?

says Antonio in *The Merchant of Venice.* Repugnance to the idea of receiving interest upon money was prevalent until the business of the world accepted the necessity; yet there are curious instances of the survival of this repugnance in our own day.

Origin of Macbeth's Ghosts

From The Oregonian, October 21, 1894

GHOSTS are phenomena of states of mind. They never exist outside the mind. They are subjective, not objective. Yet, to the mind itself, they may be the deepest of realities, like the dagger seen by Macbeth, the handle toward the hand, which to others was but his own false creation, proceeding from a heat-oppressed brain. Fancies like these forever elude scientific inquiry. Nevertheless, life is so deep a mystery, and the limits of actual knowledge are so little understood, that in many minds, perhaps in most, there is room in all ages for hallucinations.

Shakespeare's Moral Law

Address delivered by Harvey W. Scott at Portland, Oregon, June 30, 1887

WRONG can live and flourish in concealment; publicity destroys wrong. Wrong cannot abide the light, and no evil in our day long can be sure of the protection of darkness. For illustration, one may quote a passage from a speech of Richard II:

That the searching eye of heaven is hid,
Behind the globe, that lights the lower world,
Then thieves and robbers range abroad unseen
In murders and in outrage, boldly here;
But when from under this terrestrial ball
He fires the proud tops of the eastern pines
And darts his light through every guilty hole,
Then murders, treasons and detested sins,
The cloak of night being pluck'd from off their
    backs,
Stand bare and naked, trembling at themselves.

Publicity is the dread of every transgressor. Evil of every description withers under exposure. So numerous now are the means of publicity and so general is their use, that the whole moral force of organized society can be focalized at once for the suppression of evil, for the punishment of wrong. Every observer sees this done in his own time, not only in local communities, but on a world-wide scale. Thus, the people of a village reform an abuse in their municipal affairs; thus, Gladstone, thundering, in 1877–78, against the atrocities committed in Bulgaria, brought to bear upon the Turkish government the whole force of the moral opinion of mankind, which even that government was compelled to obey.

America in Shakespeare's Writings

From The Oregonian, February 23, 1902

THE all-embracing Shakespeare named America but once, and that in *A Comedy of Errors*, a play probably of composite authorship, in which Shakespeare's part is not certainly defined. He made three other allusions, that belong with certainty to America. One mentions 'still-vexed Bermoothes' (Bermudas), in *The Tempest;* the others twice name Mexico in *The Merchant of Venice.*

The discoveries of the Cabots, sailing under the English flag, beginning early in the history of American expeditions and continuing to the death of Sebastian Cabot, about the year 1557, although they gave England a footing in the Western Hemisphere which England asserted in after years, were attended by comparatively little interest at the time; for England could not do much, until the overthrow of the Spanish armada in 1588 opened the way, as Bacon expressed it, to Britain's 'commandment of the sea,' which, in Bacon's *Of the True Greatness of the Kingdom of Britain*, is stated as an essential of national power. Also, in *Of the True Greatness of Kingdoms and Estates*, Bacon said: 'He that commands the sea is at great liberty.... The vantage of strength at sea is great.... The wealth of both Indies seems in great part but an accessory to the command of the seas.'

Language Power of Shakespeare

From The Oregonian, January 30, 1898

THE English language never could have spread, as it has done, without the prodigious power of Shakespeare, on the one hand, and the colonizing and commercial activity of the Anglo-Saxon race, on the other. The language is a seamy patchwork, a linguistic crazy quilt, enlarged and extended by words from every tongue; but the genius of the language has had such assimilative energy that spoils from every source have been converted into use. Anything can be done with English by the masters, but the masters are few. Shakespeare, indeed, is the greatest master of English; and the prodigious additions made to the language, since his time, render it increasingly doubtful that the language ever will have another such master.

Slow Progress of
Shakespeare's Fame

From The Oregonian, August 20, 1888

THERE are many great books which have been slow in gaining the favorable attention of the public. Literary history is full of examples in our own time. Lewis Wallace's *Ben Hur* is an example. Many publishers refused it, and, at last, when a publisher was found, the book made way slowly. For three or four years, it was scarcely heard of. But the work has been successful, among American books, and second only to Harriet Beecher Stowe's *Uncle Tom's Cabin.*

Twelve years after Shakespeare's death, *A Midsummer Night's Dream* was played in London to empty benches. The critics pronounced it dull and tedious. When Walter Scott was in his prime, he was universally read. Twenty years after his death he was read scarcely at all. But now, as during twenty years past, he is universally read, and no one doubts that *Ivanhoe* and

Quentin Durward are immortal. Byron was
the delight of hearts for a generation; then
he fell into contempt as namby-pamby; and
now again he has a niche among the greatest
of English poets. But other writers, noted
in their day, appear to have fallen into
permanent obscurity. Who nowadays reads
Philip James Bailey's *Festus* or Martin
Farquhar Tupper's *Proverbial Philosophy?*

Wealth and Beggary in King John

From The Oregonian, March 19, 1903

HARLES W. ELIOT, president of Harvard University, says it is the greatest of all misfortunes to be born rich, and Andrew Carnegie says it is a disgrace to die rich. In the olden time the rich man was told, in *Matthew*, 'Go thy way, and sell whatever thou hast, and give to the poor, and thou shalt have treasure in heaven.' Praise of poverty takes form of fine sentiment, yet nobody thinks it an excellent thing to be poor. Human nature is little consistent in this matter. In *King John* we read:

> Well, whiles I am a beggar, I will rail
> And say there is no sin but to be rich;
> And being rich, my virtue then shall be
> To say there is no vice but beggary.

It is silly to say that it is a misfortune to be born rich, and equally silly to say that it is a reproach or shame to die rich. Indolence, indeed, may be a consequence of being born to wealth, but it is not likely to be so if wealthy parents instruct their children to a sense of their position and responsibility; but 'chill penury,' which Thomas Gray mentioned in *Elegy Written in a Country Churchyard*, cuts off the opportunity of thousands, where wealth makes one lazy or worthless.

Shakespeare's False Flattery of Antony

From The Oregonian, January 27, 1909

GUGLIELMO FERRERO undoubtedly has the right view of Antony and Cleopatra, in 'The History and Legend of Antony and Cleopatra,' which is contained in his book, *Characters and Events of Roman History*. Antony wanted money. He had dreams of political achievement, and expected to divide the Roman world with Octavianus, the future Augustus, taking to himself the provinces south of the Mediterranean and those of the Far East, and leaving to his rival those north of the Mediterranean. For this scheme he yoked with Cleopatra, whom he married, although he left behind a lawful wife in Rome. And this wife was Octavia, sister of his great rival, Octavianus. To the whole world of English readers, Shakespeare has given Antony, by far, too good a character.

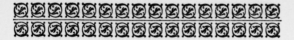

Definitions Compared

From The Oregonian, May 15, 1909

LANDER,' says the Echo *Register*, Umatilla County, Oregon, 'is a blighting sirocco.' A good definition, for the next new dictionary. Yet, one remembers that Shakespeare wrote of slander:

> Whose tongue
> Outvenoms all the worms of Nile.

And another poet, Robert Pollock, in *The Course of Time*, says:

'Twas slander filled her mouth with lying words;
Slander, the foulest whelp of sin.

John Wesley and Shakespeare

From The Oregonian, September 21, 1884

A RELIGIOUS newspaper gravely declares the belief that 'it is not probable that Shakespeare will be read enough by anybody to do any serious harm.' John Wesley was a diligent student of Shakespeare. At his death, a copy of Shakespeare's writings was found among his effects, with notes in Wesley's own hand. This was destroyed by the Reverend John Pawson, on the ground that it 'would not administer to edification.' A Methodist minister of some repute in modern days gave up reading Shakespeare, because he found himself quoting from that authority in his sermons three times as much as he quoted from the Bible.

Shakespeare and Others on Virtue

Address delivered by Harvey W. Scott at Pacific University, Forest Grove, Oregon October 14, 1903

EARNING is to be sought not for its own sake, but for useful application. Utility may be a misused word; but utility always should be kept in view. In the quick mind, any learning may be turned to account, on almost any subject. But what is the good, if one is too indolent to let it be known that he possesses knowledge? Shakespeare, who said everything, said this, in *Measure for Measure:*

Heaven doth with us as we with torches do,
Not light them for themselves; for if our virtues
Did not go forth of us, 'twere all alike
As if we had them not.

The ends of learning are usefulness and happiness. The two are inseparable. The one includes the other. Dr. Samuel Johnson, in *The Rambler*, No. 68, said:

To be happy at home is the ultimate

result of all ambition, the end to which
every enterprise and labor tends, and
of which every desire prompts the pro-
secution.

This is a proper aspiration, but without
prudence, which includes a whole family
of homely virtues — industry, perseverance,
fortitude, sobriety and the rest — happiness
forever is beyond attainment.

Sir William Hamilton, in his lecture,
Philosophy, Its Absolute Utility, Objective,
quoted with impressiveness the ancient philosopher Plavorinus: 'On earth, there is
nothing great but man; in man, there is nothing great but mind.' So, as Bacon said in
his essay, *In Praise of Learning:* 'A man is
but what he knoweth. . . . The truth of being
and the truth of knowing is all one.'[1]

He who can apply the most mental force
to problems round him, is the ablest man.
To preparation for this end, education
should be directed. This cannot be accomplished through any process of cramming the
mind with odds and ends of knowledge, but
through development of the mind. Culture

[1] *The Letters and the Life of Francis Bacon*, by James
Spedding, I, 123.

is disciplinary; not an end in itself, but a means to the acquisition and use of knowledge. Cowper, in *The Task*, wrote:

Knowledge and wisdom, far from being one,
Have ofttimes no connection. Knowledge dwells
In heads replete with thoughts of other men;
Wisdom, in minds attentive to their own.

The things one may accomplish are not in the school, however famed the name of the school, but chiefly in himself. Whether one is to profit by a school or not, will depend on what he brings to it. No school can educate a man. It can be only a helper.

Lying, in Hamlet's Day and Now

From the Oregonian, February 24, 1910

'IT is as easy as lying,' said Hamlet. Lying once was easy. Now, there are wonderful means of detection. Lying, therefore, has become a difficult expedient. A thousand agencies tend now to find out even the most ingenious person, in his attempt at deception. This is due to the spread of general intelligence, through a multitude of modern agencies. Universal use of printing, and the multiplication of books; the newspapers, scattering daily an immense variety of information, that the general mind assimilates and compares; the telegraph and the telephone; and photography and phonography; the railway and electric train service and the rural mail delivery — all these aid in detection of lying.

Morals, therefore, are advanced to a higher basis. It is useless to say there is more deception than formerly. 'Be sure your sin will find you out,' is an old aphorism,

as read in *Numbers*, but it was not as true
in the old time as now. Time was when Dr.
Frederick A. Cook could have forced his
pretense on the public, of having discovered
the North Pole. But the pretender of the
modern time is having more trouble. Abra-
ham pretended to Pharaoh that Sarah was
his sister, not his wife, and he fooled Pharaoh much longer than that expedient would
fool anybody now. The great fame and
celebrity of Odysseus, throughout the Homeric poems, rose from the poet's representation of the hero as the most accomplished
liar of the time. Driven into corners, he always extricated himself by plausible fiction.
Lying was the greatest of accomplishments,
and the poet delights that the hero was always successful.

But, in these days, lying is not so easy. So,
the pretensions and humbugs attempted by
our politicians, who pose as statesmen, now
are clearly penetrated. Some are at Washington, working for the dear people, and
bearing the labor and heat and burden of
the day, all for the dear people. It is the
rôle of politicians who, having played out
old methods, seek out for themselves new

inventions. We shall see whether the inventions are broken cisterns, that hold no water.

The aphorism, 'as easy as lying,' should be changed. It should read, 'as hard as lying.'

Glory Lost Like Antony's

From The Oregonian, July 2, 1905

MARK ANTHONY is said to have thrown away half the world to follow Cleopatra; John F. Wallace, chief engineer of the Panama Canal construction, has resigned after a year's service, and turned his back on immortal fame, for opportunities to make money through investments. Was each wise? Antony had a moment, one at least, of surcease of regret in *Antony and Cleopatra:*

> Fall not a tear, I say; one of them rates
> All that is won and lost: give me a kiss;
> Even this repays me.

Has Engineer Wallace felt no regret at resigning 'the splendid opportunities of that position, which would have made him famous the world over?' The quoted words are those of Secretary of War William H. Taft's letter of rebuke, published in the current news dispatches. Or was he, really, as he seemed to Secretary Taft, 'utterly insensible of the significance of his conduct?' In the

time to come, when a worthier genius shall
have built the canal, and Wallace shall hear
spoken the deathless name of the man who
wears the olive crown which he himself put
aside for a purse of gold, will he hear it as
Esau heard of his bartered birthright?[1]
Wallace might have walked with the im-
mortals; instead, he chose to walk with
millionaires. He might have seen his name
spurn the dull earth, as said by Nathaniel
Parker Willis, in *Parrhasius and the Captive:*

And like a steadfast planet mount and burn.

He chose instead, as in the same poem:

Like a dull worm to rot,
Thrust foully into earth to be forgot.

Mankind deals leniently with the sin of
Mark Antony; if it does not pardon, it con-
demns with pity. 'All for love, or the world
well lost,' as Dryden used the words as the
title of his Antony and Cleopatra narrative,
is folly, perhaps, but the folly of heroes. 'All
for money, or fame well lost,' may not be
folly, although Secretary Taft thinks it is; and

[1] Chief Engineers of Panama Canal construction were:
John F. Wallace (1904–05); John F. Stevens (1905–07);
George W. Goethals (1907–14).

if that be wisdom, then Benedict Arnold was wise. Next to death, history admits love, to excuse failure or crime. The account of the poet Keats, in *Endymion*, is nobler than glory:[1]

What care, though striding Alexander passed
The Indus with his Macedonian numbers?

and:

                      Juliet leaning
Amid her window flowers — sighing — weaning
Tenderly her fancy from its maiden snow,
Doth more avail than these.

[1] II, 24–25, 27–30.

Progress from Superstition
in King John

From The Oregonian, September 20, 1885

WHETHER it be true that men think less of religion than of yore, they certainly think from a different viewpoint. They are less disposed to 'religious awe,' as thus defined by Shelley in *The Cenci*, and by Wordsworth in *Farewell Light*, than their ancestors were. Men are more inclined, as the Virgilian phrase has it, to put gloomy Acheron under their feet.[1] They are all the time moving farther from that mental condition called, for want of a better word, superstition, so finely described by Shakespeare in *King John:*

This act, so evilly born, shall cool the hearts
Of all his people, and freeze up their zeal,

[1] *Felix, qui potuit rerum cognoscere causas;*
Atque metus omnes, et inexorabile fatum,
Subjecit pedibus, strepitumque Acherontis avari!
(*Georgics*, II, 490–93.)

'Happy is he who has been able to trace out the causes of things; and all fears and inexorable destiny has cast beneath his feet, and the noise of devouring Acheron.'

That none so small advantage shall step forth
To check his reign, but they will cherish it;
No natural exhalation in the sky,
No scope of nature, no distemper'd day,
No common wind, no customed event,
But they will pluck away his natural cause
And call them meteors, prodigies and signs,
Abortives, presages and tongues of heaven,
Plainly denouncing vengeance upon John.

But although men are less disposed to religious awe than their ancestors, it may be questioned whether they are less susceptible to the influences of spiritual growth and religious morality.

The Race Lesson of Othello

From The Oregonian, June 28, 1904

THE recent story of the infatuation of a white young woman for a black-amoor, and of her marriage to him, is not the first story of the kind. One has immense place in literature, and may be taken as a type or lesson of all the rest. Let our young people all read *Othello*. Many critics think that the most powerful drama ever written. Frances Anne Kemble, in her *Journal of a Residence upon a Georgia Plantation in 1838 –1839*, quoted John Quincy Adams as having remarked that Desdemona's fate was a just judgment for her marriage to a negro.[1]

[1] Mrs. Kemble's *Journal*, page 86, reads: 'Did I ever tell you of my dining in Boston, at the H——'s, on my first visit to that city, and sitting by Mr. John Quincy Adams, who, talking to me about Desdemona, assured me, with a most serious expression of sincere disgust, that he considered all her misfortunes as a very just judgment upon her for having married a *nigger?*'

PART II
Authorship of Shakespeare

Richard Farmer's Essay on Shakespeare

From The Oregonian, August 15, 1907

RICHARD FARMER'S *Essay on the Learning of Shakespeare*, first published in the year 1767, in answer to those who asserted that the works that pass under the name of Shakespeare never could have been written by 'a country clown,' stands to this day at the head of the literature which vindicates the Shakespeare authorship. The common objection, that the man whom we know as Shakespeare could not have written the works that pass under his name, Farmer dealt with in a manner which really closed the debate a century and a half ago. Yet the modern critics proceed as if there had been no experience and no knowledge, and as if they knew it all. Farmer showed, once for all, that the learning of Shakespeare was derived from the commonplaces of thought and literature about him; that his acquaintance with antiquity was wholly through translations, and at second hand; that his errors followed familiar notions prevalent in his time, yet here and there showed an insight far beyond them; that his blunders in chronology, in geography, in cosmology, were adapted from the books and the talk of his day; that in his Italian and Roman plays he used translations, yet transmuted their bald statements into immortal literary form. It seems doubtful that any person, who now worries about the 'learning' of Shakespeare, ever read Farmer's essay.

The best modern statement about Shakespeare, in small space, is an essay written by John Fiske, 'Forty Years of Bacon-Shakespeare Folly,' that appeared in *The Atlantic Monthly*, November, 1897, pages 635–52.

Why 'merciful and wonder-making[1] heaven' (the phrase is Coleridge's) created this man, none of us can know; nor why any one of us, our little atom of intelligence, was evolved out of Infinite. But it is through man that God, the Invisible, is made evident. 'God,' said Victor Hugo, in his *William Shakespeare*, Book II, Chapter I, 'creates art by man, having for a tool the human intel-

[1] See page 95, following.

lect. This tool the workman has made for himself; he has no other.' If any one marvels that the tool is a humble man like Shakespeare, a man of little learning yet of all knowledge, let him reflect that it was through this humble instrument these words were uttered, in *All's Well that Ends Well*, to wit:

> He that of greatest works is finisher,
> Oft does them by the weakest minister.

Jewels of this quality dropped continually from the tongue and pen of this marvelous man; who, besides being the greatest poet, dramatist, observer and thinker the world has ever known, was also the greatest moral writer.

First Doubt of Shakespeare's Authorship

From The Oregonian, July 15, 1888

HE question is asked: 'When and by whom were doubts first raised of the authorship of the Shakespeare plays?' It is not easy, perhaps not possible, to answer with certainty. It is probable that the controversy, about the authorship of the Homeric poems, first suggested doubts as to Shakespeare. The Homeric controversy began a century ago. Coleridge, in his lectures on Shakespeare in 1811, marveled at the prodigy of Shakespeare's works. That works of such a character should have proceeded from a man whose life was like that attributed to Shakespeare, he asserted, was the supreme wonder of literature. Possibly this hint was a suggestion to others. In one of his novels, *Venetia*, published in 1837, the late Benjamin Disraeli (Lord Beaconsfield) made one of his characters, Cadurcis, who aspired to literary criticism, say, Book VI, Chapter VIII:

And who is Shakespeare? We know of him as much as we do of Homer. Did he write half the plays attributed to him? Did he ever write a single whole play? I doubt it. He appears to me to have been an inspired adapter for the theatres, which were then not as good as barns. I take him to have been a botcher-up of old plays. His popularity is of modern date, and it may not last; it would have surprised him marvelously. Heaven knows, at present, all that bears his name is alike admired, and a regular Shakespearean falls into ecstasies with trash which deserves a niche in the *Dunciad*. For my part I abhor your irregular geniuses, and I love to listen to the little nightingale of Twickenham.

But this does not suggest the idea that Bacon was the possible or probable author. That suggestion came still later. There is a dispute as to who originated the idea in England; but in America it seems to have been suggested, first, by Delia Bacon (of the celebrated Connecticut family of that name), who published a book in 1857, entitled, *Philosophy of the Plays of Shakespeare Unfolded*, in which she sought to prove that Lord Bacon, conjointly with other writers, was the author of the Shakespeare plays. Nathaniel Holmes, of Saint Louis, published in 1866 a thick volume, *The Authorship of Shakespeare*, in which he endeavored to show that the Shakespeare plays were written by Lord Bacon.

It is hardly probable that it will ever be discovered who is entitled to the questionable honor of having first doubted the authorship of the plays of Shakespeare.

Shakespeare's Small Learning

From The Oregonian, April 19, 1886

BACON was a man of large and precise learning. He received a university education; was a Latin scholar, and wrote his principal works in the Latin tongue; traveled on the continent three years; and like Milton was an accomplished and a learned man. Shakespeare was the eldest son of a tradesman; passed a short time at a free school, but was forced soon to return to his father's business; had a wild youth; married young, and, going to London a penniless adventurer, became an actor and a playwright, and then a prosperous proprietor of a theatre.

Shakespeare's learning was so small that his plays are full of historical and geographical anachronisms. He made Hector of Troy quote Aristotle; made the Greek Theseus speak the mythology of the Goths, in *The Winter's Tale;* made a party take ship from Bohemia to Sicily, which is like taking steamboat from Helena to Portland. Of course, a man of learning, study and

travel, like Bacon, could not possibly make
these blunders, any more than Longfellow or
Lowell could violate the dramatic unities of
American history, geography and literature.

That Shakespeare was the author of the
plays that bear his name, we have authority
from his patron, Lord Southampton, who
was well acquainted with Bacon; we have
the authority of Ben Jonson, who said, in
*To the Memory of my Beloved Master, William
Shakespeare, and What He hath left Us:*

To draw no envy, Shakespeare, on thy name,
Am I thus ample to thy book and fame;
While I confess thy writings to be such
As neither man nor muse can praise too much;
'Tis true, and all men's suffrage; but these ways
Were not the paths I meant unto thy praise;
For silliest ignorance on these would light,
Which, when it sounds at best, but echoes right;
Or blind affection, which doth ne'er advance
The truth, but gropes, and urges all by chance;
Or crafty malice might pretend this praise,
And think to ruin where it seemed to praise.
But thou art proof against them, and, indeed,
Above the ill fortune of them, or the need.
I therefore will begin: Soul of the age,
The applause, delight, the wonder of our stage,
My Shakespeare rise! I will not lodge thee by
Chaucer or Spenser; or bid Beaumont lie

A little further off to make thee a room:
Thou art a monument without a tomb,
And art alive still, while thy book doth live,
And we have books to read, and praise to give.
That I not mix thee so, my brain excuses,
I mean with great but disproportioned Muses:
For if I thought my judgment were of years,
I should commit thee surely with thy peers;
And tell how far thou didst our Lyly outshine,
Or sporting Kyd, or Marlowe's mighty line;
And though thou hadst small Latin and less
      Greek,
From thence to honor thee I would not seek
For names; but call forth thund'ring Æschylus,
Euripides and Sophocles to us,
Pacuvius, Accius, him of Cordova dead,
To live again, to hear thy buskin tread
And shake a stage; or when thy socks were on,
Leave thee alone, for the comparison
Of all that insolent Greece or haughty Rome
Sent forth, or since did from their ashes come.
Triumph, my Britain! Thou hast one to show,
To whom all scenes of Europe homage owe.
He was not of an age, but for all time;
And all the Muses still were in their prime
When, like Apollo, he came forth to warm
Our ears, or like a Mercury to charm.
Nature herself was proud of his designs,
And joy'd to wear the dressing of his lines,
Which were so richly spun and woven so fit,
As since she will vouchsafe no other wit.
The merry Greek, tart Aristophanes,

Neat Terence, witty Plautus now not please;
But antiquated and deserted lie,
As they were not of Nature's family.
Yet must I not give Nature all; thy art,
My gentle Shakespeare, must enjoy a part.
For though the poet's matter Nature be,
His art doth give the fashion; and that he
Who casts to write a living line, must sweat
(Such as thine are) and strike the second heat
Upon the Muses' anvil; tune the same,
And himself with it, that he thinks to frame;
Or for the laurel, he may gain to scorn;
For a good poet's made as well as born,
And such wert thou! Look how the father's face
Lives in his issue, even so the race
Of Shakespeare's mind and manners brightly
          shines
In his well-turned and true-filed lines:
In each of which he seems to shake a lance,
As brandished at the eyes of ignorance.
Sweet swan of Avon, what a sight it were
To see thee in our waters yet appear;
And make those flights upon the banks of
          Thames
That so did take Eliza and our James!
But stay; I see thee in the hemisphere
Advanc'd and made a constellation there!
Shine forth, thou star of poets; and with rage
Or influence, chide or cheer the drooping stage,
Which, since thy flight from thence, hath
          mourned like night,
And despairs day, but for thy volume's light.

Jonson was not only a man of genius as a dramatic poet, but also a man of learning. He said also of Shakespeare:

I remember the players have often mentioned it as an honor to Shakespeare, that in his writing, whatever he penned, he never blotted out a line. My answer hath been, 'Would he had blotted a thousand,' which they thought a malevolent speech. I had not told posterity this but for their ignorance, who chose that circumstance to commend their friend by wherein he most falted; and to justify mine own candor, for I loved the man, and do honor his memory on this side idolatry as much as any. He was indeed honest, and of an open and free nature; had an excellent fancy, brave notions and gentle expressions, wherein he flowed with that facility that sometime it was necessary he should be stopped. *Sufflaminandus erat*, as Augustus said of Haterius. His wit was in his own power; would the rule of it had been so, too. Many times he fell into those things, could not escape laughter, as when he said in the person of Cæsar, one speaks to him, 'Cæsar thou dost me wrong,' he replied, 'Cæsar did never wrong but with just cause,' and such like, which were ridiculous. But he redeemed his vices with his virtues. There was ever more in him to be praised than to be pardoned.

The mystery of Shakespeare rises from the contrast of his literary genius with the lack of his scholastic training. In this respect, Shakespeare is no more a mystery than other men of great genius, who are always a puzzle to mediocrity. Cromwell was a tavern-room lounger until Charles I forced the fatal fight with parliament, and then this obscure man, who never had seen a troop in the field, until he was more than forty years of age, not only became the tactical instructor of levies, but also rose to the rank of the first strategist, soldier and statesman of his century, displaying powers for war and government equal to those of the greatest men in English history. Measured by his preliminary training, Cromwell is as unaccountable, as much of a mystery, as Shakespeare. Can we account for Burns, Lord Clive, Washington, Napoleon, Bismarck, Shelley, Keats, Patrick Henry, Gambetta, Franklin, Lincoln, Greeley, for any man of genius, by the training of the schools?

Men of genius do not date from schools of

learning. Genius is a law unto itself. The rare genius of observation, imagination and contemplation is the mystery of Shakespeare. His very lack of severe scholarship helped him; learning might have repressed his spontaneity, crippled the free, natural motion of his eagle-winged spirit, just as a severe scholastic training probably would have spoiled Burns for such work as *Tam o' Shanter*, *The Jolly Beggars*, *The Banks of Doon* and *Highland Mary*. Instead of poetry, full of the fragrance of the wild rose, full of the voices of the wood thrush and the mountain brook, we should have had a writer of polished, elegant verse, like Gray; beauty in brocade, lacking soul.[1]

[1] "I do not think Gray a first-rate poet. . . He was a mechanical poet." Boswell's *Life of Johnson*.

Did Shakespeare Know
the Law?

From The Oregonian, November 8, 1903

T the annual meeting of the Vermont Bar Association, October 27, 1903, at Montpelier, the president, John H. Senter, delivered an extended address, entitled, 'Was Shakespeare a Lawyer?' He went into the subject with thoroughness, and reached the conclusion that what the writer of Shakespeare's plays did not know about the law would fill a volume, while what he did know could be put into a paragraph.[1] The dramatist had heard some law terms, in discussion of his father's affairs in court, for the elder Shakespeare was at the wrong end of several cases. The dramatist had picked up a few phrases from lawyers who hobnobbed with the London players, and several words, now exclusively used by lawyers, were in the common language of the people in Shakespeare's time. Mr. Senter said:

[1] The Senter address is published in *Proceedings* of the Vermont Bar Association (1903), and covers 60 pages.

Shakespeare uses legal words and phrases many times in his plays, and often uses them correctly; and it is also true that in some of the plays there is little, if anything, that indicates any knowledge, technical or otherwise, of the law. . . . It was not necessary for a man of Shakespeare's genius to have been a lawyer, a doctor or a sailor, a butcher or a theologian in order to have written these great works of his, that will live through all time.

The Vermont speaker went into details. He asserted that 'Shakespeare's misuse of legal terms was frequent and flagrant.' For example, in the seventeen cases of the use of the word 'dower' only one was correct. So, also, Shakespeare's use of 'indenture' and 'moiety,' of 'distrained' and 'testament,' was wrong, and his use of 'arrested on the case,' in *The Comedy of Errors*, was altogether wrong, since this action, in the sense there indicated, was not known in England until nine years after the play was written. The description of the trial of the Duke of Buckingham, given in *Henry VIII*, was admitted to show a familiarity with legal procedure and technical terms, but any argument that might be founded on that is void, because the legal phraseology is taken almost literally from Edward Hall's chronicle, *The Union of the Two Noble and Illustrate Families of Lancaster and York* (1542). If any one's legal standing is affirmed by that passage, it is Hall's, not Shakespeare's. Most of the legal phraseology, in the historical plays, comes from the chronicles of Hall and Holinshed.

In *The Merchant of Venice*, it was shown that a more flagrant illustration of ignorance of the law of Shakespeare's own time, hardly could have been presented. The proceedings had no foundation in common law, statute law or moral law. The man who wrote that scene not only had no legal training, but described proceedings that could not possibly have occurred in any court of law.[1] But Bacon was a great lawyer; so, the assertion that there is no law in Shakespeare is a sort of negative pregnant against the claims of the Baconians.

[1] The Senter address says: 'The only saving clause therein for Shakespeare's legal acumen is that he put this law into the mouth of a woman, and not that of a man.'

Myriad-Minded Shakespeare

From The Oregonian, February 15, 1879

UNDER this heading, *Appletons' Journal*, February, 1879, prints an article, in which certain new objections are stated to Shakespeare's authorship. The writer is not devoted to the idea that the plays were produced by Bacon; although he thinks Bacon may have produced some of them, and perhaps Raleigh others, while possibly both and possibly neither had a hand in them. But, he asserts, 'whoever did, the statement that William Shakespeare did not, tallies with all the internal evidence of the plays themselves.'

Right here is one of the main proofs by which the Shakespeare authorship most surely can be maintained. Through the plays are marks of a single, mighty hand. It is evident that but one writer was doing such wonderful work. And that it was Shakespeare, is established by contemporaneous evidence. But, says the *Appletons'* essay:

Let any one try to conceive of the busy manager of a theatre, who succeeded by vigilance, exact accounting, business sagacity and prudence, in securing and saving not only a competency, but a fair fortune; in the meantime, while engaged in this engrossment of business, writing Isabel's magnificent appeal to the duke's deputy, Angelo, or Cardinal Wolsey's last soliloquy! Or conceive of the man who gave the wife of his youth an old bedstead and sued a neighbor for corn delivered, penning Antony's oration above Cæsar, or the soliloquy of Macbeth debating the murder of Duncan, the invocation to sleep in *Henry IV*, or the speech of Prospero, or the myriad sweet or noble or tender passages that nothing but a human heart could utter! Let him try to conceive this, and his eyes will open to the absurdity of the belief that these lines were written by the lessee and joint manager of a theatre, and he will be satisfied in his own mind that no such phenomenon is reasonable probable or safe to have presented itself.

This is simply an attempt to try the foremost man of all this world by ordinary rules. There is no use trying to 'conceive this,' as the writer suggests, for Shakespeare is inconceivable. Coleridge, profoundest of critics, called him 'an oceanic mind,' in *Table Talk* (March 15, 1834), and exclaimed, in *Lectures on Shakespeare* (1818), at end of section II:

Merciful, wonder-making Heaven!
What a man was this Shakespeare. Myriad-minded, indeed, he was.

And, again, in *Biographical Literaria*, chapter XV, Coleridge spoke of 'the greatest genius that, perhaps, human nature has yet produced, our myriad-minded Shakespeare.'

We know clearly Shakespeare's relations with his theatre; and it is not more difficult to conceive that he should have written these works under such conditions, than that he should not have written them. For here was the greatest phenomenon in the intellectual history of mankind, who excelled all others in minuteness of perception and vastness of grasp, in delicacy of touch and sweep and subtlety of thought; and the work he produced is just such work as would not be elaborated from the scholarship of the closet. It came from his associations with men and his observations of human life, and thus was a registration of all his forces. Bacon, Raleigh and other men of the time, great as they were, exhibited in their known writings no such intellectual powers. The characteristic style of Shakespeare has no imitators. In his plays there is much, indeed, that is commonplace, and could have been produced by other hands; and, doubtless, considerable parts were thus produced, since we know that playwrights of the time often worked together on the same piece. But in the plays, which go under Shakespeare's name, there are passages constantly occurring which could not be mistaken for the work of any other hand, and the chief dramas, as *King Lear*, *Hamlet*, *Macbeth* and *Othello*, are the sustained work of this most mighty of all creative minds.

Shakespeare was known intimately to Ben Jonson, Marlowe, Peele, Fletcher, Carew, Beaumont, Donne, Selden, Cotton, Greene, and the whole galaxy of play writers of the time. These men of wit and intellect not only never questioned his powers, but also bore testimony to their unrivaled variety.

He was not of an age, but for all time,

said Jonson. In such company, the impos-
ture, presupposed by the Shakespearean
myth notion, would have been impossible.
If he was only a copyist for other hands,
where is any other work comparable with
this, which those other hands produced?
Again, study of the plays in chronological
order furnishes a mirror of the development
of one transcendent mind; so that the internal evidence of the plays themselves, instead of disproving their accredited authorship, is really the strongest of all affirmative
arguments.

Beaumont, in a letter to Jonson, thus
spoke of the meetings of the contemporary
wits and poets at the famous Mermaid Club:

What things we have seen
Done at the Mermaid! heard words that have
    been
So nimble, and so full of subtle flame,
As if that every one from whom they came
Had meant to put his whole wit in a jest.

Shakespeare had wonderful powers of wit
and conversation, strong friendships and
melancholy dissatisfaction with his work and
opportunities. He was held in affectionate
esteem by his intimate friends. He was re-

garded as a man of honesty and integrity. The sonnets probably reflect his thoughts and feelings more than do any other of his works, and reveal his tender sensitive nature.

Appleton Morgan's Book on Shakespeare Authorship

From The Oregonian, January 1, 1882

IN a book, *The Shakespearean Myth*, by Appleton Morgan, a member of the New York bar, the author says that the man named Shakespeare, who was born on the banks of the Avon 300 years ago, did not write the works attributed to him. Many essayists have endeavored to give the glory of Shakespeare to another, of whom Alexander Pope said in *An Essay on Man:*

> If parts allure thee, think how Bacon shin'd,
> The wisest, brightest, meanest of mankind.

But Mr. Morgan's work, nevertheless, is substantially original. Those who preceded him relied upon internal evidence; he examines the question from purely external evidence. They bent their energies to the task of establishing the claims of Lord Verulam. He does not aim so much at setting up any other man, as in pulling down Shakespeare. True, he suggests one who did write

the plays, but he does not much insist upon
the nomination which he makes to fill the
vacancy, occasioned by the transformation
of the reputed author into a mere myth.
What he does insist upon is that there is a
vacancy. The result is an uncommonly
interesting book, a valuable contribution to
the literature of Shakespeare. Nay, it is
more. Mr. Morgan is a lawyer. When he sat
down to write, doubtless he was in the same
habit of mind as when, having received a re-
tainer, he sits down to prepare a brief. And,
as an argument of a lawyer, retained against
Shakespeare, the book appears clever and
plausible enough, not certainly to induce the
jury to give him a verdict, but perhaps to
cause one or two in the panel to disagree
with their obstinate associates.

Mr. Morgan makes an elaborate argument
to prove that Shakespeare was merely a
jack-of-all-trades about a theatre, and not
the ideal poet, philosopher and seer. We
have not space to present the points of
his argument, many of which are strong,
and all of which are ingenious. But we are
much mistaken if he shakes the faith of the
jurymen. They will be likely to remind

Mr. Morgan that Shakespeare was in undisturbed possession of his fame for three centuries, a strong presumption against the contrary argument. They will be likely to say that Shakespeare was a genius. Of this Mr. Morgan takes little account. 'A presumption 300 years old,' Mr. Morgan remarks, 'may be a strong one to overthrow. But if its age is all there is of it, if it only be strong in years, it can be toppled over.'

It is improbable that the fame of Shakespeare would attain so great an age without a truthful origin. Our author's summary attempt to dispose of this matter, is the weakest part in the book. We have said that Mr. Morgan did not lay sufficient stress upon the consideration that Shakespeare, if he did write these plays, was a full-orbed genius. His argument would be weightier if Shakespeare was an ordinary man, talented, but nothing more. Could a butcher's apprentice, a preacher, produce dramas, and, as Ben Jonson says, be —

not of an age, but for all time?

Certainly not, if he was merely a man of talents. Yes, if he was a genius. For it is true, that, to a supreme genius, all things are possible. Such a person knows all the royal roads to learning. His intuition, perception, assimilation — who shall set a limit to them?

We have the testimony of Ben Jonson, a fellow play writer, of John Heming and Henry Condell, his associates in London, and the first publishers of his collected works, as well as of other contemporaries, as to the amazing extent and versatility of Shakespeare's powers. True, the record leaves much to be desired. But, Mr. Morgan is disposed to deprecate this testimony, rather than give it just and full weight. We may regret that we have not more, but that should be no reason for undervaluing what we have.

That Shakespeare was a thrifty theatrical manager, Mr. Morgan admits no doubt. As such a manager, it is suggested that he was editor, and not author, of the contributions of ambitious amateurs or plodding playwrights, who were driven to their wits for support; and that he 'farmed out his name to these, just as the original Farina farms out his to makers of delectable water of Cologne.' But, against this theory, the insuperable objection lies that the alleged plurality of writers of the Shakespearean dramas could not have performed this composite labor. It is well known that the author made free use of the materials of preceding playwrights. On the other plays, again, it is all but certain that two or more writers worked together.

A reader, who has studied these productions until his mind is saturated, can not fail to sift out the work of the master hand. There was only one writer capable of producing such work, and his authorship no one can mistake. Bacon's acknowledged work shows that he was totally incapable of Shakespeare's authorship. With all Bacon's mighty range of observation and facility of expression, he was far below Shakespeare. Take his *New Atlantis* as a work of imagination, and compare it with *The Tempest*, and see the gulf between the philosopher and the play writer. Mr. Morgan's theory, that the Shakespearean drama was written by a dozen or more persons acting in concert, such as Southampton, Raleigh, Essex, Rutland, Montgomery and other fine gentlemen, including a 'needy and ambitious scholar named Bacon,' is ingenuous and, to a great extent, original. But this theory of collaboration is nullified by the clear evidence that all the characteristic work of the plays proves one authorship. The Shakespearean mode of expression is inimitable.

From The Oregonian, October 4, 1885

Mr. Morgan imagines a great wonder, which involves the coöperation of many kinds of talent in the creation of a literary mosaic, of which Othello and Falstaff, Ophelia and Beatrice, the Fool in *King Lear*, and Justice Shallow are the components. But, if a genius could not have drawn these characters from the open volume of human nature and from his own imagination, it is certain that a syndicate of less gifted writers could not.

The authors of that era are well known. Their works have survived, as those of the minor writers of the period. Some of them were men of great learning, of high poetical power, of varied gifts. But none of them produced a single work that can be compared with any of Shakespeare's. All the Marlowes, Dekkers, Beaumonts, Jonsons, Fletchers and

Chapmans, added together, could not match the towering excellence of Shakespeare.

In many of Shakespeare's dramas are commonplaces which may have been written by other hands. But no reader, who enters into the spirit of Shakespeare, will mistake for anything else that has come from the brain of man, the characteristic work of the master. Other men may have had his quickness of perception and his range of observation, but none has had, with these gifts, Shakespeare's variety, facility, fulness, accuracy, originality and general power of expression, his depth of reflection, his power to arrange facts of observation and knowledge. The dramas that go under Shakespeare's name, it is possible to believe, were produced by a genius, gifted beyond ordinary intellects with superlative intuitions and with capacity for absorbing knowledge from every source; a poet in the best sense of the word. It is not possible to believe that the man who produced the works which we know as Bacon's, great as they are, could also have produced these different and higher works called Shakespeare's; nor is it possible to believe that these works were written by a club or syndicate of unknown writers.

So-Called Cipher of Bacon

From The Oregonian, January 10, 1902

THE Bacon cipher, alleged to have been discovered in Shakespeare, has no relation to the subject-matter of the dramas, and is based on the manner in which they are printed. It is not a word cipher, but made up by typographical devices, that is to say, by different fonts of type. One finds letters here and there, in fonts different from the font of the general text, and, putting them together, he gets words and sentences; and these words and sentences contain strange revelations. They are said to show that Bacon claims the authorship of the Shakespeare dramas; that Bacon was the son of Queen Elizabeth and the Earl of Leicester, and left the record of his birth in this cipher, with many other wonderful things. But this method of printing was used only in the first collected edition of Shakespeare's plays, known as the first folio, which edition, it is assumed for the purpose of this revelation, was edited, letter by letter, by Bacon himself, since no one else could be let into his secret, which, however, he trusted posterity might discover.

All this is sufficiently fanciful and fatuous. One may prove in the same way that Bunyan wrote *Paradise Lost*, and that Milton wrote *Pilgrim's Progress*. One, moreover, may prove anything else he seeks to prove, of either work, by use of different fonts of type in printing the texts. But, how happens it that the type of the first folio of Shakespeare has these peculiarities? Types then were clumsily made, and the typographical art, as one may see from books of that time, was a wonderful hodge podge. Different fonts often were intermingled, and every page had a piebald appearance. It is shown that this same cipher method can be derived from early editions of Ben Jonson's plays, from Robert Burton's *Anatomy of Melancholy*, and from divers other books of the time.

Besides, in this new Baconian revelation, the differences in the fonts are often so obscure, if they exist at all, that only the microscope can detect them; and such differences frequently might be the consequence of injury to type that had been used more or less.

This new 'discovery,' therefore, seems the clearest product of literary lunacy yet developed among the devotees of the so-called Baconian theory.   One accepts the theory; he assumes as facts certain things he wishes to prove; and then he proceeds to pick up letters here and there from the pages of the author, selecting letters or words printed in type that shows peculiarities and differences, to prove them.   One can make up in this way any story he requires; and the task is especially easy if one uses books that were printed 300 years ago.

Donnelly's Myth of Shakespeare

From The Oregonian, July 2, 1887

IGNATIUS DONNELLY is author of an article in the June, 1887, number of *The North American Review*, pages 572-82, entitled 'The Shakespeare Myth.' Mr. Donnelly was in Congress from Minneapolis for several years; he had considerable fame at one time as a 'red-hot' stump orator, and his article shows that he has read much and writes well, that is, he writes in good literary style. He says that Shakespeare could not have written the plays, because they reveal great learning. Bacon was the most learned man of his age, while Shakespeare had no education in boyhood, save that of a village school. Hence, Bacon wrote Shakespeare's works.

It may be answered that, while the plays of Shakespeare display wide knowledge of men and things, they do not display great learning; there is no evidence in the plays, Mr. Donnelly to the contrary, that 'the

writer was a master of Greek and Latin,' or
Spanish or Italian or French. The French
passage in *Henry V* could have been written
easily by Shakespeare, at the dictation of
another. The Latin is legal Latin, or such
familiar phrases as any reading and observant man to-day readily picks up and uses,
without having studied the classics. There
is no evidence in the plays that the writer
knew the Greek language. George Chap-
man's *Iliad* and Plutarch's *Lives* were ample to furnish all the knowledge Shakespeare
manifests of Greek and Roman mythology
and history. The Italian novels that he
adapted to his purpose, even as English playwrights to-day adapt French plays to their
stage, could have been translated for him
by any one of Shakespeare's scholarly friends
like Jonson or Sidney. Rabelais, the French
poet, was popular in England at this time,
and there are some indications that Shakespeare had read him or heard him read,
but there are no marks in the plays of the
large learning of a scholar.

Nor do we see ground for Donnelly's assertion that 'the writer was a lawyer.' The
plays have no more technical phraseology of

the law than any observant man of the world
of to-day, meeting lawyers, dropping into
courts, absorbing all kinds of conversation
from all kinds of men, could pick and use
correctly. One may as well say that Shakespeare must have been a jockey, because he
correctly defines the points of a good horse;
or a doctor, because he accurately describes
certain diseases, or must have known
and practiced a hundred other callings,
mechanical, mercantile and professional, as
to say he must have been a lawyer. He
had the eyes, the ears, the observation, the
memory, the concentration, the faculties of
apprehension, absorption and assimilation
that are comprehended in a man of genius;
and, above all, he was a man of poetic imagination who could put himself in any place
and time. He was not more wonderful, as a
contemplative genius in all these respects,
than Napoleon as a practical genius. Napoleon, without much reading or experience,
solved every problem as fast as he met it, to
the admiration of the ablest and most learned
men of his court. When we remember that
Shakespeare was a poet and philosopher, not
a soldier, Shakespeare seems no more a mys-

tery than Napoleon, except so far as poetic genius is loftier and rarer than military genius.

Does Mr. Donnelly suppose that Bacon would have been so loose in his grammar as Shakespeare? Does he suppose that a grave, austere mind, of metallic eloquence, like Bacon's, could have created Falstaff, Ariel, Mercutio, Rosalind, Romeo, Juliet? Intellect and knowledge were supported for this work by an imagination, an experience and a temperament that no more resembled the traits of Bacon than the singing flight of the skylark resembles the voice and motion of a stately dray horse.

The absence of any manuscript remains of Shakespeare is not remarkable, since most persons know what Donnelly does not seem to know, that the Globe Theatre, in which were all Shakespeare's papers, was burned to ashes. The dissolute boyhood of Shakespeare is not more inconsistent with his subsequent renown, than the boyhood of many men of genius with their mature fame. The resemblance of occasional words, phrases and even thoughts on the plays to utterances of Bacon, is of no consequence, for Shakespeare took rough ore from everybody, high and low, ancient or modern, smelted out the gold and gilded with it his own splendid genius. If we say Shakespeare never wrote the plays that are attributed to him, to whom shall we attribute them? Surely not to Bacon, who, with all his intellectual endowments, lacked the power that God in his grace gave to Shakespeare, the splendid imagination of a great poet.

From The Oregonian, September 13, 1887

Ignatius Donnelly can find but two poems that are attributed to Bacon, and while these are of doubtful historical authenticity, no man can call them by any other name than rhymed prose, and very platitudinous prose at that. The Boston *Herald* shrewdly says:

> Perhaps the most improbable thing of all is that a mind like that of Bacon, so competent to appreciate their value, could have been indifferent with regard to claiming them as his own.

The fact that we know comparatively few details of Shakespeare's life, is accounted for when we remember that he always manifested extreme indifference to the fate of his plays and poems. He never alluded to them; never superintended their publication; his life was devoted to making money; his ambition was to be a landed gentleman in his native town, and when he attained that, he at once retired content to his estate. Of course, Shakespeare was neither drunkard nor loafer, for drunkards and loafers did not rise from youthful poverty to affluence, in the conduct of the theatre during the reign of Queen Elizabeth and James I, any more than they do in our own day. Whether Shakespeare was dissolute for his day, there is no historical evidence; he was at least convivial, as were the men of his time, without disgrace, or even discredit. If somebody should dispute the authenticity of Byron's grand and reverent apostrophe to the ocean in *Childe Harold's Pilgrimage*, canto 179, on the plea that Byron was a man of immoral life, we should have an assumption not a whit more absurd than the plea that, because Shakespeare was probably fond of tarrying long at the wine with Ben Jonson, he could not have written Hamlet's soliloquy.

Richard Farmer's essay, written a century ago, comparing the text of the plays with Plutarch, showed plainly that Shakespeare was not a classical scholar. Shakespeare appropriated his plots and often his text from others, just as the elder Dumas did, when he bought a scribbling fellow's work, recast, rewrote it and turned, by the touch of his Midas fingers, dross into pure gold. To prove Shakespeare a man of learning from his plays, is impossible; to prove the contrary, by citation of anachronism, is easy. That Shakespeare was a bad man, is open to grave historical doubt; that Bacon was a bad man, is open to no historical doubt. So that the inconsistency of serious immorality, with the possession of high genius, is no more glaring in the one case than in the other; and, therefore, ought not to be urged as a ground for incredulity, as to the authentic authorship of the plays.

The cipher theory is not original with Donnelly; he has adopted only the theory of Delia Bacon, published by her more than thirty years ago, and reiterated by Mrs. Ashmead Windle, of San Francisco, in 1881.

So far as occasional identity of thought

and expression is concerned, between Bacon and Shakespeare, it is sufficient to say that a man who used what suited him from Plutarch might stoop to pick a johnny jump-up in Bacon's garden, and turn it, by a touch, into a pansy. If one will read Coleridge's famous *Hymn in the Vale of Chamouni*, and then read *Chamouni at Sunrise*, from the German of Friederike Brun, he will see an identity of thought and even of expression which can be explained only on the presumption that Coleridge, like Shakespeare, knew how to appropriate and adorn.

Examples of Cipher Parallels

From The Oregonian, October 25, 1887

NE of Ignatius Donnelly's methods of establishing the claim that Bacon wrote the Shakespeare plays, is the evidence furnished by what Donnelly calls 'parallel passages.' This is an old device, which was worked years ago for a great deal more than it was worth by Nathaniel Holmes, of Saint Louis. A large number of Donnelly's parallel passages are given by the New York *World*, and, from their quality, it is clear that Donnelly's work in this line is inferior to that of his Saint Louis predecessor.

For example, Mr. Donnelly holds that, because Bacon said 'golden world' and Shakespeare said 'golden age,' an identity of authorship is shown; apparently, because he can not understand that two men should use such an unusual word as 'golden.' The words 'gentle,' 'fantastical,' 'excellent,' 'moment,' 'top' and others, appear in Bacon and Shakespeare, and this is said to prove identity. Thus Bacon said 'the gentle dew'; Shakespeare, 'the gentle rain.' We hear now and then of 'gentle zephyrs,' even, and of 'gentle shepherds,' all stolen from Bacon, of course. Bacon said 'excellent music'; Shakespeare said 'excellent voice'; and in both we hear of a 'quiet conscience.' Could books with those words be written by different men?

But there are yet worse identities in these parallel passages. Bacon spoke of a buried man, as returned to 'his mother, the earth.' Shakespeare also called the earth man's 'mother.' This proves, not only that Bacon wrote Shakespeare's plays, but also that he invented the legendary part of the Roman history, for when Lucius Junius Brutus went to consult the oracle, with the sons of Tarquin, they were told that he who should first kiss his mother should reign in Rome; and Brutus, when he went out, fell down and kissed the earth, because the earth is the true mother of us all. But it is proved not only that Bacon invented Roman history; he wrote also Paul's epistle to the Corinthians. For example, Shakespeare said: The queen 'died every day she lived.' Mr. Donnelly said: 'It is nothing to find Bacon and Shake-speare using such words as "day" and "dead" but it is significant when we find both writers using them in connection with the same curious and abstruse thought, to-wit: that individuals metaphorically die daily.' As this curious and abstruse thought first appears in Paul's epistle, and is a famil-iar part of the burial service, a New York literary paper asks, 'did Bacon write these?'

Mr. Donnelly's main fault is lack of the literary sense. He looks merely upon the limbs and outward flourishes of a literary work, not upon the inner parts. Another fault is the small range of his information, especially as to the English language and literature. He says that coincidences of ex-pression 'occur not in the ordinary words of our language, the common bases of speech, without which we cannot construct sen-tences or communicate with each other, but in ordinary words employed in extraordinary and figurative senses.' He imagines this because he does not know that certain words in Shakespeare which, having acquired new meanings, and now sounding odd to us in the relation in which Shakespeare used them, were in his time the common words for the case presented. Mr. Donnelly says, 'We find both Bacon and Shakespeare using the unusual word "disclose" for "hatch."' It was not unusual at all. It was the common correct term of that time. Mr. Donnelly similarly is muddled over Hamlet's 'a nipping and an eager air.' He calls 'eager' 'a curious word, used to describe the coldness of the air.' It is not curious, when the origin and early use are considered. It is the Latin word *acer*, 'sharp,' 'keen,' but comes into the English language through the French, and in the French form, *aigre*, which means (of the air) 'sharp,' 'piercing.' The same word is in 'vinegar,' sharp (sour) wine. To say that the air is sharp with cold, is commonplace in all languages. In another place, Shakespeare uses 'eager' for 'sour.' The word now has passed almost wholly out of the old meanings, as applied to inanimate things, and is used chiefly to describe the desire with which the mind longs for or pursues an object.

A moderate course of primary study, in philology and literature, should be recommended to the Donnellys before they attempt to annihilate Shakespeare.

Donnelly's The Great Cryptogram

From The Oregonian, May 9, 1888

MR. DONNELLY makes his cipher say what he wishes it to say about Bacon, Cecil, Marlowe and others; he makes it describe Shakespeare as an utterly worthless fellow, a man of no capacity or character; 'a poor, dull-spirited, greedy creature,' so given to debaucheries that 'yet in his youth he is written down old, with all the characters of age.' Thus, the very terms, in which some of the characters produced by Shakespeare are delineated, are employed by Mr. Donnelly to characterize Shakespeare himself. A word-picker, running over the range of the Shakespearean vocabulary, assembles and arranges words and forms them into sentences that give the results he seeks. However, in the delineation thus obtained of the life and character of Shakespeare, he is directly contradicted by the positive testimony of Shakespeare's contemporaries and intimate friends.

It is evident that Mr. Donnelly has performed a great deal of labor upon his book, *The Great Cryptogram* (1887). But it is labor of the most fruitless kind. He has made a story, indeed; but so can any other story be made out of Shakespeare or any other author, by the like method. A reviewer says:

It is plain from his method that Donnelly first found the statements that he wanted to find. He then hunted (probably in a concordance of Shakespeare) till he found the first word, or some other word of his proposed phrase. By then counting backward or forward, up one column and down another, or down one column and up another, sometimes counting hyphenated words as two and sometimes as one, by adding or subtracting at his own sweet will, and by other false and transparent devices, he collected the words that form his phrase or narrative. He did this by no apparent rule, while alleging that he has a key to the cipher which he refuses to reveal at last, having in view he says, the publication of future books which he fears to impair in interest, if he divulges the only thing that would make this book of interest or value.

Here let one fitly exclaim —

O, most lame and impotent conclusion!

PART III
Miscellany on Shakespeare

Shakespeare Among
Great Authors

From The Oregonian, December 27, 1886

 LETTER from Monmouth, Oregon, says that the members of the class of literature in the state normal school have asked their friends to select six authors of highest excellence and fame, with special mention of the best works of each author; and they have requested the editor of this newspaper to join in making the selections. The class, we are told, consists of twenty-five young men and women of Oregon, Washington, and Idaho.

In our opinion, four names are supreme in literature, and after these four the choice of the two others may be made from fifty or more authors, according to the tastes of the person who makes the selections.

The four supreme names are Homer, Dante, Cervantes, and Shakespeare. Doubtless, there are persons who would name others as fit for this great company. But it is not likely that any considerable number of such persons would agree as to others, and their disagreement would show the unapproachable eminence of the leading four. Although these four are supreme, yet standing round their thrones are others, mighty indeed.

Homer is as a great fountain whose stream is traceable through all the great works of the human mind. History, poetry, art, fiction take their rise in him; in him are the elements of the drama, both tragedy and comedy; in him are high questionings as to human life and human destiny, springing from a sense of the nobility of man and yet full of the idea that man is an instrument in the hands of a higher power. The *Iliad*, as a poem of heroic action, has never been equaled. It abounds in touches of nature only surpassed in number, yet not in fidelity, by the hand of Shakespeare. The *Odyssey* remains the world's greatest romance; it is the source of wonderful tales, of remarkable stories of adventure in the borderland between the realms of fact and fiction, the natural and the supernatural. A sense of the debt of the world's literature to Homer grows in proportion to one's increasing knowledge of the world's literature and of Homer himself.

The place in literature held by any one of the four supreme writers is unlike that of the others, except for eminence. Neither Dante nor Cervantes nor Shakespeare is like Homer. Each took the materials he found about him, wrought upon them in his own way, and gave the result the stamp of his own personality. It is beyond doubt, however, that the transcendant works of Dante and Cervantes are not so readily appreciated by the Northern or the Anglo-Teutonic or the American mind as those of Homer and Shakespéare. Their methods are not so natural. They do not agree so closely with northern conceptions of life, of duty, of destiny. We do not always see their scope and meaning easily, because we do not fully understand the mental conditions which produced their works. For comprehension of the *Divine Comedy*, much labor and pains are necessary; first, to catch the spirit and purpose, and second, to get an understanding of the author's methods of blending old materials with later events. The right understanding requires not only a general but

also a special culture. This problem places
Dante somewhat out of range. But by the
suffrages of all men of eminence in criticism,
Dante's name is one of the very first in literature. From the small company of the highest authors he cannot be excluded.

Cervantes, also, is *sui generis*. He is more
easily understood than Dante; but his work
does not at once make the impression of
greatness upon the reader. At first, his work
seems more absurd than useful, more amus-
ing than profound; but like other great books
Don Quixote grows upon one through life.
What at first was but a ridiculous story
fills with deeper meaning, and, as the reader's
acquaintance with men and affairs widens,
he sees in this unique production one of the
first creations of genius.

Shakespeare's incomparable name it is
necessary only to mention. After we have
named these four, the next group would contain such names as Æschylus, Plato and
Thucydides; Vergil, Cicero and Tacitus;
Bacon and Milton; Goethe, Schiller, and
Heine. Just where we should place such
writers as Tasso, Molière, Ben Jonson,
Dryden, Pope, and many others of former

centuries, or where we should place Byron, Scott, Victor Hugo, and others of the present century, will depend upon variety of taste and judgment; and, again, opinions will differ as to the best works of any foremost writer. Young readers should read as widely and carefully as possible of the best authors; or, as a guide thereto let them take any good historical outline of literature. There are excellent histories of each of the great literatures: Greek, Roman, French, German, Spanish, Italian, and English. Wider reading will carry one into some account of Persian, Indian, Arabic, Scandinavian and other literatures. In all this, careful study of the spirit of Hebrew literature, of course, should be included.

Religious Source of the English Drama

From The Oregonian, December 11, 1904

THE morality play was one of the early forms of the English drama. It followed close upon the mystery plays, religious in their conception and development; for the drama, like every other form of literature and art, rises out of the religious nature of man and is but an expression of the 'divine thrusting on' in human nature. The drama in Greece had a similar religious origin. So in France. So in Germany. English drama is no exception. Four centuries ago, when the English drama was passing out of the representation of religious mysteries into personification of secular ideas, the morality play appeared. Through secularization of the drama, the morality play developed as a substitute for the miracle play; thence it passed on into the wide human scheme of the predecessors of Shakespeare, and, finally, into the mighty Shakespearean masterpieces.

The main source of the English drama was the liturgy of the church, and in the course of time the term 'mystery' was applied to the religious service of any of the great festivals of the calendar, and even to the services of the church in general. These exercises passed imperceptibly into a kind of dramatic representation. It was natural enough that at religious festivals or anniversaries important personages and events should be represented in visible form, with such details as either Scripture, legend or the imagination of the author could supply. An idea may be formed of these old religious dramas from the titles of such of them as have been preserved; among them *The Creation of the World*, *The Fall of Man*, *The Story of Cain and Abel*, *The Crucifixion of Our Lord*. Clear traces of the universality of these dramas may be found in early works of sculpture and painting, yet extant in Europe.

From this first stage the drama passed into another kind of representation, entitled a 'morality.' *Everyman* is a type of this form; and although not the earliest, it is among the earliest that have been preserved entire, and the only morality that is generally known. It was produced and published about four centuries ago. It is printed entire in the first volume of Hazlitt's edition of *A Select Collection of Dodsley's Old English Plays*. This great and simple tragic masterpiece has been called 'The noblest conception of death presented by the imagination of the Middle Ages.'

'The subject of this piece,' says Dr. Thomas Percy, referring to *Everyman*, 'is the summoning of man out of the world by death, and its moral, that nothing will avail him but a well-spent life and the comforts of religion.'[1] Everyman refers to every member of the human race. Death delivers his message to Everyman, who at once appears upon the scene, and tries in vain by pleas and bribes to turn the summoner away. He applies in vain to Fellowship and Kindred, but they successively forsake him. Finally, he calls to mind one other friend whom he has loved all his life, Goods, who surely will prove true to him in his distress. But Goods, in the presence of this enemy, can do nothing.

[1] From Percy's 'On the Origin of the English Stage,' in his *Reliques of Ancient English Poetry*.

Everyman betakes himself to Good Deeds, who, after upbraiding him with his long neglect, introduces him to her sister, Knowledge, who leads him to the holy man, Confession, who gives him a scourge called Penance. This Everyman inflicts upon himself on the stage, and then withdraws to receive the sacraments from the priest. On his return he begins to wax faint; and after Strength, Beauty, Discretion and the Five Wits, each personified in the drama, have taken their final leave of him only Knowledge and Good Deeds remain. Everyman gradually expires on the stage. Knowledge hears the singing of angels, and Good Deeds is summoned by an angel to follow the soul of her master to heaven.

Most of the old plays of this class in English have been lost. The most notable ones that have been preserved have been made accessible to modern readers, through Dodsley's collection. They afford an extremely interesting study of language and forms belonging to the transitional period of English — the time when it was passing out of archaic into modern forms.

One of the earliest moral plays in the

English language known to exist is *The Interlude of the Four Elements*. Therein, the popularization of science is attempted through theatrical representation of the old notion of four elements, earth, air, fire and water, of their supposed qualities and properties, and of the generation and corruption of things made of the mixture of them. The persons of the drama are allegorical, who one after another attempt to set forth ideas of astronomy and cosmography. The play portrays the conclusions that 'the earth must needs be round, that it hangeth in the midst of the firmament, and that it is in circumference above 21,000 miles.' This is exceedingly curious, since it precedes the first circumnavigation of the globe, and, by more than twenty years, the publication by Copernicus of his system of astronomy, which first announced the planetary system and the place of the earth. For still another reason, the piece has a curious interest. It is the first writing in English in which the name America appears. The date of the composition is approximately fixed by an allusion to the discovery of the West Indies, 'within this twenty year.'

Relics like these are valuable chiefly to students of the history of literature. The whole subject, embracing all periods of English, has been treated by many writers. The literature of the subject is voluminous, and grows continually. Scholars in the universities of Great Britain, America, France and Germany are expending great labor upon it. Even the catalogues of the new publications are immense; and it is not likely that the literature of any language has been more deeply explored than our own.

Hasty Errors of Great Authors

From The Oregonian, November 26, 1909

CONTENTION of several critics over the use of words and idioms in English, retouches an old subject, but one whose discussion yields little profit. Two recent letters deal with such phrases as 'I had rather be,' and 'I had rather not do it.' One writer insists that such phrases are incorrect, and he would substitute 'would rather' for 'had rather'; while the other maintains that since great writers have used 'had,' in such phrases, this form therefore is allowable. Texts from Scripture, Shakespeare and Chesterfield are produced in support of this last contention.

Undoubtedly the form was used early in our language, or it could not have found a place in the English Bible. Use of it by Shakespeare is not especially significant; for so great a writer as he is above all rules. It would be an act of wonderful temerity to take the liberties with language that Shakespeare took, or to try to imitate his peculiar

turns of thought or expression. The rule
may be laid down that it is not wise to copy
the inadvertencies and errors committed by
great writers in their haste, or to maintain
that they establish the canons of the language. In a thousand instances Shakespeare
was grossly ungrammatical. Burke and
Byron and Johnson often were.

Walter Savage Landor, one of our very
great writers and critics, in the third volume
of his *Imaginary Conversations*, deals with
this very same phrase, 'I had rather,' etc.
The 'conversation' is between Samuel Johnson and John Horne Tooke. Landor makes
Tooke pester and worry the great khan of
literature no little. 'Permit me,' said Tooke,
'to ask whether we can say, *I had hear?*'
Johnson: 'You mean to say, *heard.*' Tooke:
'No; I mean the words, *I had hear.*' Johnson: 'Why ask me so idle a question?' Tooke:
'Because I find in the eighth chapter of
Rasselas, *I had rather hear thee dispute*. The
intervention of *rather* cannot make it more
or less proper.' Johnson: 'Sir, you are right.
I hope you do not very often find such in-
accuracies in my writings.'

Not a soul among us should attempt to

imitate great authors, or to take the error
of great authors as guides or excuses for our-
selves. Who, for example, would follow this,
from *The Tempest*, as good and proper gram-
matical writing?

> Full fathom five thy father lies;
> Of his bones are coral made.

You will not find the like in so correct a
poet as Tennyson. But no editor accuses
Shakespeare, or alters his text.

> But Shakespeare's magic could not copied be;
> Within that circle none durst walk but he,

said Dryden in the prologue to *The Tempest*.
Now don't get into a dispute because 'but
he' ought to be 'but him.' The poet of that
line was a great author also. But you
shouldn't attempt to imitate him. You will
fail, if you do. And the grammar of these
verses, from Byron's *The Prisoner of Chillon*,
don't you try to imitate or to criticize, or the
poetry, either:

> My hair is gray, but not with years,
>> Nor grew it white
>> In a single night,
> As men's have grown from sudden fears.

Of course you will not try your hand at the poetry, because you are powerless and mute. Let the grammar alone, too, and don't imitate it, and don't profess to believe that is the law of language.

Incorrectness may be pardoned in great writers. But it is better to pass such errors unnoticed than to imitate or repeat them, or to insist on their correctness.

Brief Comments on Shakespeare

From The Oregonian, December 25, 1883

THERE is a self-seeking which is also benevolence, but it is inspired by religion, which gives to man's heart, what, it has been said, the Creator gave to Shakespeare's mind, many sides, so that he feels the joys and the sorrows of the human race.

From The Oregonian, October 2, 1887

The inimitable, free, flowing Shakespeare, who surpassed all writers of English! Milton recognized this in *L'Allegro*, where he speaks of Shakespeare's —

Native wood notes wild.

From The Oregonian, January 1, 1888

The character of Mrs. Malaprop did not originate with Sheridan, for Shakespeare is full of her kind of comedy.

From The Oregonian, February 5, 1888

The test of a great play is not the power shown in spots or in a single character, but in several or many characters; in the evidence of the myriad-mindedness of the author. Submitted to this test, while Hamlet may be Shakespeare's greatest work in the delineation of a single character, *Hamlet* is not his greatest play. . . . Measured on all sides, the judgment that *Henry IV*, rather than *Hamlet*, *Macbeth*, *King Lear* or *Othello* is Shakespeare's greatest play, will stand the test of time.

From The Oregonian, July 22, 1888

There is scarcely a great author who does not give examples of wordplay. Shakespeare is fuller of them than any other writer.

From The Oregonian, September 11, 1892

Shakespeare gathered unto himself the intellectual wealth of an era and was the greatest plagiarist by right of his greatest genius.

From The Oregonian, August 18, 1895

To criticise the language of the English Bible would be as absurd as to criticise the language of Shakespeare and Milton, on the ground that their human and superhuman heroes speak the artificial dialect of poetry, rather than that of vulgar humanity.

From The Oregonian, August 1, 1897

Even the seers are the most laborious workers. The pages of Shakespeare, illumined with vision of nature possessed by few and with insight into the human heart shared by none else, are crammed with evidence of information so various that only extensive research could have developed it. The secrets of all arts, the methods of all professions, the principles of all sciences, ministered to his hand.

From The Oregonian, January 25, 1903

Shakespeare holds the important place, together with the English Bible, in the study of English.

From The Oregonian, November 30, 1904

On one side of his life, man is but a part, usually an indistinguishable part, of a vast machine. But he is more than the bee or the ant or the beast of the jungle, nevertheless.

He has a personality; there is reserved in him,
as Hamlet says —

>   Some quantity of choice.

From the *Oregonian*, *January* 29, 1905

Nature requires us to work, but has ways
of punishing excesses in that direction, too. If
she does it in no other way, she makes success
useless, for her wreath often covers hair that
has grown gray, and fame comes when the
hearts it should have thrilled are numbed.
The greatest of all moral writers has said in
The Merchant of Venice —

They lose it that do buy it with much care.

From *The Oregonian*, *April* 9, 1905

In the *Book of Job*, as in *Hamlet* and *Faust*,
the problems of the universe are found in-
scrutable. So it is in all great literature. All
the more reason, then, for avoidance of dog-
matics.

From *The Oregonian*, *January* 26, 1908

Homer, Dante, and Milton used materials
that lay about them. So did Shakespeare.
But they had not Shakespeare's supreme

power of penetration into the secret springs of the human mind.

From *The Oregonian*, *July* 25, 1908

There was collaboration in the making of numerous plays, in which Shakespeare had a hand. To the reader who has caught the Shakespearean spirit, it is clear at once where the work of the poet paramount begins and where it ends.

Index

Index

Folios, Shakespeare, 43, 44.
Folklore, religious, 7; use by
Shakespeare, 20–22.
Fool, in *King Lear*, 104.
Forum, The, cited, 13.
France, Shakespeare's small
knowledge, 20, 110; dram-
atists, 22; defeated by
Black Prince, 23; war with
Henry V, 24, 25; words in
English, 120; literature,
129; drama, 130, 135.
Franklin, Benjamin, genius,
88.
Furness, Horace Howard,
Shakespeare scholar, 41.

Gambetta, Leon, genius, 88.
Georgics, by Vergil, 72.
German, Frederike Brun,
poet, 116.
Germany, literature, 129;
drama, 130, 135.
Ghosts, mental, 50.
Gladstone, William Ewart,
statesmanship, 52.
Globe Theatre, London,
burned, 112.
Gloster, in *King Lear,* quoted,
32.
Goethals, George W., en-
gineer, 70.
Goethe, Johann Wolfgang
von, dramatic power, 7;
greatness, 128.
Gordon, George, Lord Byron,
see Byron.
Goths, mythology, 83.
Gray, Thomas, poet, 59, 89.

Great Britain, sea power, 54;
colonies, 55; cited by Ben
Jonson; James I, 86, 114;
Charles I, 88; drama, 135;
see England and Britain.
Great Cryptogram, The, by
Ignatius Donnelly, 122.
Greek, Shakespeare's small
knowledge, 20, 85, 110;
Theseus, 85; literature, 129;
drama, 130.
Greeley, Horace, genius, 88.
Greene, Robert, contempo-
rary of Shakespeare, 96.
Greenfield, property man in
Henry V, 44, 45.

Hale, Sir Matthew, view on
money interest, 48.
Hall, Edward, chronicle,
source of Shakespeare, 92.
Hamilton, Sir William, on
mind and matter, 64.
Hamlet, type character, 13,
14, 141; dramatic unit, 29;
on lying, 66; soliloquy, 114;
'eager air,' 120.
Hamlet, drama, greatness, 7,
8, 96, 141; characterized
by Algernon Charles Swin-
burne, 12; Ophelia, 104;
soliloquy, 114; 'eager air,'
120; quoted, 122, 130, 143.
Harris, Frank, author, 13.
Harvard Classics, Dr. Charles
W. Eliot, compilation, 8.
Harvard University, Charles
W. Eliot, president, 58.
Haterius, Roman jurist, 87.